CONSTRUCTION AND HOUSING IN THE WEST BANK AND GAZA

The West Bank Data Base Project

The West Bank Data Base Project is an independent research group established in 1982 to study and analyze demographic, social, spatial, legal, economic and political conditions in the West Bank and Gaza. The project, which is directed by Dr. Meron Benvenisti, is funded by the Rockefeller and Ford foundations and administered by The Brookings Institution, Washington, D.C. A continuously updated, computerized data base and its own research are the basis for the project's publications, including maps showing present and projected developments in the region.

About the Author

Dr. Bahiri is engaged in research in the economics of peace between Israel and its neighbors and in the analysis of the future consequences for the involved parties. He has published widely on these subjects. Formerly, Dr. Bahiri was with the Armand Hammer Middle East Cooperation Project of Tel Aviv University.

CONSTRUCTION AND HOUSING IN THE WEST BANK AND GAZA

Simcha Bahiri

WESTVIEW PRESS
Boulder • San Francisco • Oxford

The West Bank Data Base Project

This softcover edition is printed on acid-free paper and bound in library-quality, coated covers that carry the highest rating of the National Association of State Textbook Administrators, in consultation with the Association of American Publishers and the Book Manufacturers' Institute.

Published in 1989 in Israel by The Jerusalem Post, POB 81, Jerusalem 91000, Israel

Published in 1990 in the United States of America by Westview Press, Inc., 5500 Central Avenue, Boulder, Colorado 80301, and in the United Kingdom by Westview Press, 36 Lonsdale Road, Summertown, Oxford OX2 7EW

Library of Congress Cataloging-in-Publication Data
Bahiri, Simcha.
  Construction and housing in the West Bank and Gaza / by Simcha Bahiri.
    p. cm.
  "West Bank Data Base Project"—Verso of t.p.
  ISBN 0-8133-7982-2
  1. Housing—West Bank. 2. Housing—Gaza Strip. 3. Construction industry—West Bank. 4. Construction industry—Gaza Strip.
I. West Bank Data Base Project. II. Title.
HD7358.45.W47B34 1990
338.4'76908'095695—dc20   90-12250
                                                                      CIP

Printed and bound in the United States of America

  The paper used in this publication meets the requirements
  of the American National Standard for Permanence of Paper
  for Printed Library Materials Z39.48-1984.

10   9   8   7   6   5   4   3   2   1

Table of Contents

Appendices

List of Tables

1. Introduction, Acknowledgements And Objectives Of The Study

1.1 Introduction

The State of Israel has reached a fairly high standard of housing and construction activity on a per capita basis as compared with the remainder of Mandatory Palestine – e.g. the West Bank (WB) and Gaza Strip (GS) (or both WB/GS). Nevertheless, the gap has narrowed since the occupation in 1967. Prior to that they had been under Arab occupation (Jordanian in WB, Egyptian in GS).

It is the intention of this study to review both past housing and construction developments, and their present state in the West Bank and Gaza Strip, as well as to assess under various political-economic scenarios the potential for developing this sector of the economy over the coming decade: 1987-1997.

There has been a paucity of reports dealing with housing and construction activities in the West Bank and Gaza Strip. This is in marked contrast to industry, in which a sister-report[1] by the author was partially based on other studies. No research works involving independent field work have been identified apart from reports of the statistical offices of Jordan[2] and Israel[3].

With the exception of the pre-1967 period covered by the Economic Planning Authority[4], the majority of the data has been based on statistical samples compiled by the Israeli Central Bureau of Statistics[5]. As their data deals only with building and construction for the Arab residents (i.e. excluding Jewish settlements and "military installations"), some distortion results from the period of the initial occupation to the present. Furthermore, most works [6] involving the extrapolation of economic potential published over the last decade have been based on a single scenario (Bahiri, 1984 and 1987 is an exception[7]) of a continuation of occupation or of the establishment of a Palestinian state with an economy separate from that of Israel[8]. This study will deal with several options and sets of data.

1.2 Acknowledgements

The author wishes to acknowledge the assistance provided by the director of the WBDP, Dr. Meron Benvenisti, who made many useful suggestions, and his contribution based on previous studies published by the WBDP. The author also acknowledges the help of his typist, Mrs. Sally Maroko, who corrected many errors, and of his wife, Doreen, both for her patience and her help in proofreading.

1.3 Objectives

The objectives of this work are therefore:

i. To outline the state of the construction sector of the economy and its part in development in the WB/GS based on statistics from various sources;

ii. To describe both barriers and catalysts to development of housing and construction;

iii. To assess the dependence of the construction sector of the Territories on Israel;

iv. To determine present housing conditions and future needs;

v. To project potential economic development scenarios and their consequences for construction under various possible political-economic options; and

vi. To provide Israeli and Palestinian planners and/or decision-makers with information to assess consequences of various alternatives.

2. Methodology, Projections And Statistical Notes

As in all research projects, a variety of approaches has been used in meeting the objectives of this study. Broadly these have included both inductive and deductive methods.

Statistics for the pre-1967 situation in the Territories were mainly based on the 1967 reports of the Israeli Economic Planning Authority[1]. The main source for developments from 1967 to the present is the publications of the Israel Central Bureau of Statistics (CBS)[2]. Little else has been published. Note, however, that we will concentrate only on relevant data pertaining to the indigenous or Arab sector in the West Bank and Gaza both for their actual state and their potential development. East Jerusalem will be excluded because Arab building there is not listed separately in Israeli statistics[3]. While there is some question as to the accuracy of the statistics, particularly as regards population, official statistics of the CBS will for the major part be used[4]. Whenever useful, data will be combined or separated to generate more meaningful indicators.

One of the major ideas in this work is the generating of alternative economic, population and construction projections for 10 years hence. These are based on the most optimistic outcome of three different but possible scenarios, namely:

i.   a continuation of the pre-uprising (or pre-intifada[5]) situation and occupation, and hitherto existing trends in the territories - e.g. no major change of policy by Israel (or Jordan) and no major local major demographic or building shift (i.e. a conservative scenario);

ii. a continuation of the occupation, albeit with a granting of some degree of autonomy and/or a renewed Jordanian participation, and an easing of restrictive economic barriers and constraints with a consequent

3

improvement in the "quality of life" (i.e. a reformist scenario);
iii. a separation of the West Bank and Gaza Strip from Israel, either in the framework of a Palestinian-Jordanian confederation or as an independent Palestinian entity (i.e. a radical scenario).

The 1987 data was calculated by extrapolating 1986 statistics and by available recent partial indicators. Thereafter three separate projections are generated for the following decade to 1997. All three projections involve the maximum growth-rate possible for each scenario over a 10-year period. The present "intifada" was ignored for this illustrative purpose.

There has been no special report on construction either by the CBS or others in the WB/GS. Many of their tables have been combined and/or "creatively" analyzed[6]. Original tables have been checked by and discussed with other economists and specialists for their coherence, reliability and objectivity – particularly those dealing with various future scenarios. While there were differences of interpretation with other analysts, the author is reasonably sure of the validity of the (possible) overall trends shown, given a relatively surprise-free (e.g. other scenario) future.

A full list of bibliographical sources can be found in the reference notes for each chapter.

4

3. Background: 1948-1967

3.1 Israel

Even prior to the establishment of Israel in 1948, Jewish and Arab areas of what was then Palestine were largely split into two semi-autarkic economies[1]. With the establishment of the State, despite a total hiatus with the West Bank and Gaza Strip, Israel was left with a sizeable Arab minority (170,000) in areas under its control. As most of the Arab population in the early years of the State was in areas under military government, the degree of economic integration (labor, trade, services) was initially limited. From the late '50s to 1966, with the lifting of military government, the Arab sector of Israel become increasingly united with that of the Jewish economy – despite the continuing social hiatus[2].

Under various pretexts, Arab agricultural land was taken over by the Jewish State and settlers and the Arab laborers reduced to wage labor in the Jewish sector, often physically distant from their homes. This influx of wages was to aid in gradually raising the economic status of Israel's Arab population.

Quite early in the State's history, Arab labor began to replace Jewish labor in the construction sector. In the 1950s and early '60s, this reached some 30 per cent of total Israel Arab labor and of total labor in the construction industry[3]. The percentage of Arab labor in the construction industry was double their percentage of the work force. Another strong connection of Israeli Arabs with construction is that their rate of increase of housing units (measured by number of households) was higher, after the period of mass Jewish immigration, than the corresponding rate among Jews between 1957 and 1967[4]. Despite a lower standard of living in the Arab community they had a propensity to building based on their savings – much of it from work in the Jewish construction sector. Methods learned there were also transferred to the Arab construction sector.

The gap in the per capita gross domestic product (GDP)

between the Jewish and Arab sectors narrowed between 1949 and 1967, but a considerable gap remained, and still remains[5].

The State of Israel developed its GDP at a rate of 10 per cent per annum from 1949 to 1967, despite the recession of 1964-1967, with an investment (gross domestic capital formation) growth rate of nearly 6 per cent per annum[6].

Development in the Arab sector, with its emphasis on private consumption and investment in housing, did not lag significantly behind the Jewish rate of development, but significant differentials continued. Nevertheless, it was an uneven development dependent more on employment in the Jewish sector than on real economic development. This was to be repeated with the occupied Territories after 1967.

3.2 The West Bank

With the establishment of Israel and its expansion to nearly 21,000 sq. km. of territory during the War of Independence, a total hiatus occurred between it and the residual territories. These territories, comprising the Arab Triangle (as the West Bank was known) and the Gaza Strip, occupied between them the remaining 6,000 sq. km. The major part or well over 90 per cent of this residual area remaining under Arab control was occupied and eventually annexed by Hashemite Transjordan, which thereby transformed itself into the Kingdom of Jordan.

Although this heartland of Arab Palestine considerably lagged behind the Jewish sector in construction and economic development, it (the West Bank) maintained a higher level of social and economic development than that of the East Bank (former Transjordan)[7].

A part of the large refugee population fleeing areas occupied by Israel went both to the West Bank and (increasingly) to the East Bank. The share of Jordan's population in the West Bank declined from 50 per cent in 1952 to about 40 per cent in early 1967[8]. While this caused a strain on the economy of the West Bank and a lower rate of construction, this influx of a more advanced population resulted in rapid economic development of the East Bank. Furthermore, in practice, despite the granting of Jordanian citizenship to West Bankers, there was considerable discrimination in

6

allocation of economic and construction projects and their rate of development lagged behind that of the East Bank[9], and certainly of Israel.

In the wake of the 1948 War and with the occupation by Jordan of the West Bank, construction was brought to an almost complete standstill. This was to continue until the early 1950s when much building in the newly established refugee camps took place.

In 1965, per capita expenditure on housing needs for all of Jordan (East and West Bank) was one-eleventh that in Israel; and the level of the West Bank was lower than the Jordanian average[10].

There is a direct relationship between income level as measured by per capita private consumption and housing consumption. This is shown by Table 3.2.1 which compares these for Jordan and Israel for the years 1962 to 1965[11].

Residential dwellings in the West Bank in 1961 had much fewer basic amenities (such as running water in dwellings, electricity, separate kitchen, separate bathroom and internal toilet) than found in Israel – even for its Arab minority. Some data for this is shown in Table 3.2.2. This is because the rate of development of these facilities among Israel's Arab population was higher than the corresponding development in the West Bank. Table 3.2.3 illustrates the differences in these amenities for the West Bank between the cities and the villages. The latter may be imputed from the difference between the data for the entire West Bank and for the cities.

The bulk (70 per cent) of investment for the West Bank for the years 1962 to 1965 was for housing[11] (with 10 per cent for other construction and 20 per cent for equipment). Furthermore, the proportion of housing in the West Bank and the proportion of construction workers in the West Bank were higher than in the East Bank in 1965[12]. Nevertheless, because of their smaller population, the area of building which reached nearly 150,000 sq. m. in 1965 for cities in the West Bank, excluding East Jerusalem, averaged only 35 per cent of total building area for cities in Jordan between 1962 and 1964[13]. The major part of that construction was for housing and it consisted mainly of buildings with only one housing unit. Building consumed 140,000

7

tons of cement, which was imported from the East Bank[14].

Statistics from the September 1967 census in the West Bank show that there were 226,000 rooms in the West Bank and a further 28,000 in East Jerusalem – a total of over 254,000 rooms. In May 1967[15] there were 845,000 inhabitants in the area thus resulting in a crowded 3.3 persons per room. An area of building of an estimated 200,000 sq. m. (including villages and East Jerusalem) per annum was therefore insufficient to meet the housing needs of the population.

Nearly 95 per cent of the households[16] in 1961 in the West Bank were permanent buildings of which over four-fifths were of stone, one-eighth of cement or cement blocks, and one-ninth of mud.

Around 40 per cent of the total market or sales value of houses built is value-added, the rest being purchased materials and resources excluding labor[17]. The number of workers employed in West Bank construction was nearly 18,000 in 1961 and rose rapidly to around 22,000 in 1965. In addition, there were around 3,000 workers in the building material industries[18].

In 1966, there were some 20,000 workers in building excluding public works but including East Jerusalem and the villages[19]. The area built was nearly 200,000 sq. m.[20]. Thus each worker built 10 sq. m. This was one-fifth the amount each Israeli worker built. Cohen[21] states that in 1961 the West Bank efficiency rate was one-tenth of that in Israel, but he understates the West Bank building area.

In 1966, 140,000 tons of cement, all imported from the East Bank, were consumed in the West Bank with a population including East Jerusalem of 845,000. The per capita consumption was, therefore, 166 kg. as compared to over double that in Israel.

According to a Bank of Israel report quoted by Lipshitz[22], just prior to the Six Day War it took over 200 workers in the West Bank to generate a value of IL 1,000,000 while in Israel this took less than 50 workers – i.e. less than one-quarter.

Much of the building just prior to the war was by families themselves with little outside assistance, and thus not reflected in employment figures[23].

"Per capita GNP in Israel was, in 1965, six times the per

Table 3.2.1

Private and Housing Consumption in Israel and Jordan: 1962-65
(in current Israeli Lirot – 1 Jordanian Dinar equals IL 8.40)

	1962	1963	1964	1965
Per Capita Housing Consumption				
Israel	250	310	360	430
Jordan	45	45	45	45
Per Capita Private Consumption				
Israel	1,930	2,200	2,460	2,800
Jordan	480	525	540	570
Percent Housing Consumption of Private Consumption				
Israel	13	14	15	15
Jordan	9	8	8	8

Source: Israel: Central Bureau of Statistics
Jordan: Statistical Year Book, 1965

Table 3.2.2

Per cent of Families with Selected Basic Facilities (1961 and 1963)
West Bank and Israel

	Running Water in Dwellings	Electricity	Separate Kitchen	Separate Bathroom	Internal Toilet
West Bank (1961)	12	13	31	7	24
Israel (Non-Jews-1961)	–	–	40	11	21
Israel (Total population-1963)	93	93	86	81	85
Israel (non-Jews-1963)	38	31	47	14	28

Source: Israel: Central Bureau of Statistics
West Bank: Jordanian Census of Population and Housing, 1961

Table 3.2.3

Percent of Households in West Bank Cities with Selected Facilities Inside Dwelling in 1961

	Entire West Bank	Jerusalem	Rammallah El-Bira	Bethlehem Beit-Jallah Beit-Sahur	Nablus	Tulkarem	Hebron
Kitchen	31	69	53	51	66	61	41
Bathtub	7	11	23	8	30	24	10
Internal Toilet	24	80	34	33	87	54	61
Electricity	13	49	43	41	60	42	23
Running Water in Dwelling	12	26	21	6	73	57	18

Source: Jordanian Census of Population and Housing, 1961

capita GNP of the West Bank"[24] which indicated the relatively underdeveloped state of that area. Construction in the West Bank was labor-intensive, backward and mostly in the private sector of the economy. By 1967, it had not met the objective requirements of its society.

Much of the above-mentioned stagnation in West Bank construction was the result of the lack of any significant planning initiatives under Jordanian rule. The West Bank and Gaza Atlas[25] indicated that while the "Jordanians amended some Mandatory outline city plans and prepared plans for the newly-created municipalities," they made "no changes in the regional planning schemes." Furthermore, as these plans were not "based" on topographical maps, infrastructure and the road system could not be developed. "Areas for housing development were extended, but without the necessary public services...Town development during this period was dictated not by regulations and densities determined in the plans, but by the realities of land ownership and economic viability."

Table 3.2.4

Distribution of Gross Domestic Product in the West Bank – 1966

	Million Jordanian Dinar	Per cent
Agriculture	14.4	27.1
Industry	4.7	8.8
Construction	3.4	6.4
Electricity and Water	0.8	1.5
Transportation	2.0	3.8
Trade	10.3	19.4
Finance	0.7	1.3
Housing (imputed)	4.7	8.8
Public Services	7.2	13.5
Other Services	5.0	9.5
Total	53.2	100.0

Source: Economy Planning Authority, Jerusalem 1967

Table 3.2.5
Uses and Resources in the West Bank and Jordan – 1966

	JORDAN		THE WEST BANK			ISRAEL
	Million Dinar	Percentage Breakdown	Million Dinar	Percent of Jordan	Percentage Breakdown	Percentage Breakdown
Resources						
Gross Nat.Product	196.5	89.3	68.2	34.7	89.5	90.5
Import Surplus	23.6	10.7	8.0	33.9	10.5	9.5
Total Resources	220.1	100.0	76.2	34.6	100.0	100.0
Uses						
Private Consumption	150.3	68.3	51.3	15	67.3	61.1
Public Consumption	39.8	18.1	14.4		18.9	19.7
Gross Capital Formation	30.0	13.6	10.5	35.0	13.8	19.2
Total Uses	220.1	100.0	76.2	33.9	100.0	100.0

Source: National Planning Authority, Jerusalem 1967

3.3 The Gaza Strip

The 365 sq.km. of territory known as the Gaza Strip were occupied by Egypt during Israel's War of Independence in 1948. Unlike the West Bank, which was annexed to Jordan, this residual area was formally held by Egypt, officially in trust for the Palestinians, pending the establishment of their state. The Gaza Strip, as a result of the war and Egyptian occupation, was cut off from its natural hinterland. In 1948, due to the vast influx of refugees, comprising more than half the population, and its relative isolation, it was nearly on the point of collapse when it was taken over by the Egyptians.

However, it was separated from Egypt by the semi-desolate Sinai peninsula. The Strip was never integrated into the Egyptian economy and thus remained a separate and distinct entity. It had no natural resources except limited underground water supplies. Since Egypt was administering the Strip on a "temporary" basis, long-term development plans were not possible. Private initiative was the major source of investment in the economy. What little development existed was concentrated in agriculture. Construction accounted for just 6.2 per cent of the GDP (see Table 3.3.1) despite the objective need of resettlement generated by the massive refugee population. Furthermore, what little development took place was largely unbalanced[26]. On the eve of the Israeli occupation, the per capita income was only 27 dinars – half that in the West Bank.

Table 3.3.1 also shows the sources of income and distribution of employment in the Gaza Strip in 1966. Note that construction involved 6.2 per cent of the GDP (E£ 1,000,000) and roughly the same percentage of employment (4,000 employed). Investment in construction was some E£ 2.5m. which represented 60 per cent of total investment in the Strip in 1966[27].

The Gaza Strip in 1966 had over 440,000 inhabitants, of which some 72 per cent were refugees. Gross domestic product in construction was around E£ 1m.; consequently, per capita expenditure was only E£ 2.25. Construction labor was not listed separately[28] but included in the 15,000 in the category: trade, personal services and construction. It was imputed that the proportion of construction labor was the same as its share in the GDP and this resulted in an estimated 4,000 employed[29]. The GDP, or value-added, per employed person was therefore E£ 250 in construction – a fraction of that in Israel.

Of the E£ 4m. in investment in 1966, E£ 2.5m. (or 60 per cent) were in construction, mostly private. This was around 14 per cent of the GNP (see Table 3.3.2).

Thus, the Gaza Strip construction sector, while playing a part in investment, was nevertheless relatively undeveloped on the eve of the Six Day War (1967).

Table 3.3.1

Sources of Income and Distribution of Labor in the Gaza Strip in 1966

Source	Millions of Egyptian Pounds	Percent of Total Income	Percent of GDP	Employment	
				Thousand	Per cent
GDP by Sector					
Agriculture	5.5	26.2	34.4	22	35.0
Industry	0.7	3.3	4.4	2	3.2
Construction	1.0	4.8	6.2	4*	6.3
Trade & Personal Services	4.3	20.5	26.9	11*	17.5
Transport & Communication	0.5	2.4	3.1	4	6.3
Administration & Public Services	4.0	19.0	25.0	20**	31.7
Total	16.0	76.2	100.0	63	100.0
Transfers from Abroad					
UNRWA and other Public Transfers	4.0	19.0	–	–	–
Remitted from Abroad	1.0	4.8	–	–	–
Total	5.0	23.8	–	–	–
Income from all Sources	21.0	100.0	–	–	–

* Bregman, Economic Growth, p. 69; Trade Services balance of 15,000
** includes 10,000 in Palestine Liberation Army

Source: "The Economy of the Gaza Strip and Sinai." Economic Planning Authority, Jerusalem, 1967

Table 3.3.2

Resources and Uses in the Gaza Strip in 1966

	Millions of Egyptian Pounds	Percent of Resources	Per cent of GNP
Gross National Product	17.5	57	100
Imports of Goods & Services	13.0	43	74
Total Resources	30.5	100	174
Private & Public Consumption Investment (GNCF)	18.4	60	105
(of which construction was E£ 2.5m.	4.0	13	23
Export (and Expenses of Foreigners)	8.1	27	46
Total Uses	30.5	100	174

Source: Cohen, 1986

4. Housing And Construction Under Occupation: 1967-1987

4.1 General

The West Bank and Gaza Strip were occupied by Israel in the June 1967 War. A process of creeping annexation began which, 21 years later, had transformed Israel and the occupied Territories into a *de facto* bi-national entity (see Appendix 2).

Initially with the occupation, up to 250,000 refugees[1] fled to Jordan from the West Bank. In addition, over the next two to three years the population declined further as more inhabitants emigrated. The population in September 1967, (according to the only census the Israelis took in the Territories), of the West Bank (excluding East Jerusalem which was annexed by Israel) and Gaza Strip was 596,000 and 390,000 respectively. In 1970, this was 608,000 and 370,000 respectively, i.e. a slight decline in the total population. During these three years Israeli policy was formulated. Van Arkadie states that:

"Every Israeli cabinet since 1967, while insisting that there will be no return to the June 1967 borders, has decided not to decide the political future of the West Bank and the Gaza Strip. But Labor Government policy, including economic policy, was grounded in three understandings: Israel would not formally annex the territories; Israel would not withdraw from them; and Israel would not allow them to become a net economic burden."[2]

The 1968 breakdown of resources and expenditures shows the effects of the war (see Table 4.1.1) with investment accounting for less than 8 per cent of the GDP. Note that private expenditure alone exceeds the GDP and that the import surplus is 40 per cent. The economies of the West Bank and Gaza in 1968 were in dire straits both because of previous neglect and due to the effect of the war.

During the first decade of occupation and integration, under the Labor Government, economic ties between Israel and the Territories developed, but fell short of maximum integration. In fact, the government encouraged the "open bridges"[3] policy which allowed relatively free movement between the West Bank and Jordan. Furthermore, for the most part Jewish settlement and construction were limited to certain less-populated areas, e.g. the Jordan Valley[4].

The employment of laborers in Israel generated a considerable transfer of earnings to the Territories, much of which was used for housing. In 1977, the Territories represented less than 7 per cent of the GNP of Israel. For Israel, the Territories (excepting for WB/GS construction labor) were of marginal significance. For the WB/GS, Israel was an economic colossus.

Not all writers were to take such a beneficent view of Israeli economic policy. Hilal[5] argued that a colonial-type relationship was developing with three types of exploitation – in trade, monetary relationships and exploitation of the labor force.

It was generally agreed that the Territories were becoming more closely integrated with Israel. Despite the rise in the material standard of living, much of it due to earnings in Israel, growth was uneven. Although industry stagnated, both agriculture and construction grew rapidly. It is the development of this construction sector that we will subsequently concentrate on.

Bregman[6] of the Bank of Israel, in reviewing the five-year period 1968-1973, states that there was extremely rapid growth with a per annum rise of real GNP of 18 per cent. The growth rate far exceeded the pre-1967 period. He argues that: "The rapid and continuous growth of the areas' economies must be attributed to the close ties established between them and the Israeli economy. The abrupt removal of the barriers that had separated the two economies' populations and prevented trade between them, created in fact a common market of three economies: those of Israel, the West Bank and the Gaza Strip."

It should, however, be emphasized that part of the rapid increase is due to the low base of 1968 when the Territories had not yet fully recovered from the effects of the war.

With the change of government from Labor to Likud after the 1977 elections, new policies aimed at accelerating the integration of the Territories into Israel (both politically and economically) began rapidly to take effect[7]. This was especially true of Jewish settlement in the West Bank in areas which were previously ignored. Increasingly, land was taken over by the Israeli State and other Jewish bodies. By 1985[8], such land amounted to 52 per cent of all land in the area. The number of Jewish settlers in the WB/GS at the end of 1987 reached 67,000[9], which is still only 1.7 per cent of the total Jewish population and 4 per cent of the population of the Territories excluding East Jerusalem.

For a variety of reasons, the rapid growth of the Territories' GNP, averaging 12 per cent per annum during 1968-77, declined drastically between 1977 and 1984 to around 4 per cent[10] per annum. Between 1980 and 1986 there was near zero growth in the GDP (0.5 per cent annually). Investment declined and official unemployment reached 4 per cent, as against 1 per cent earlier. The statistics suggest a stagnant, undeveloped economy with the greatest "developmental" factor being the large migratory labor force now over three-eighths of the work-force. In Gaza alone, it is approaching half their active work-force.

In some ways, Israel may be viewed as the core economy and the occupied Territories as the colonial or peripheral economy. Both economies may now be viewed on one hand as systems in their own right and on the other as sub-systems of an increasingly single-system economy.

Table 4.1.1

1968 Expenditure on Gross Domestic Product in the West Bank and Gaza Strip (NIS in thousands, 1980 prices)

| | WEST BANK | | GAZA STRIP | | WB + GS | |
	NIS.000	% of GDP	NIS.000	% of GDP	NIS.000	%of GDP
Private Consumption	1537	120.6	614	95.9	2151	112.2
Public Consumption	240	18.8	145	22.6	385	20.1
Investment	73	5.7	73	11.4	146	7.6
Resources	1850	145.2	832	129.4	2682	139.9
Import Surplus	576	45.2	1899	29.4	765	39.9
GDP	1274	100.0	643	100.0	1917	100.0

Source: Statistical Abstract of Israel, 1969

Table 4.1.2

1986 GDP, Employment & Productivity in Israel, the West Bank & Gaza Strip*

	ISRAEL		WEST BANK		GAZA STRIP		WB / GS		WB/GS as % of Israel
	$ mill.	%	$ mill.	%	$ mill.	%	$ mill.	%	%
Gross Dom. Product**	27,550	100.0	1,177	100.0	314	100.0	1,491	100.0	5.4
Agriculture	1,653	6.0	386	32.8	69	22.0	455	30.5	27.5
Industry	6,888	25.0	92	7.8	41	13.0	133	8.9	1.9
Construction	2,204	8.0	166	14.1	70	22.3	236	15.8	10.7
Services	16,805	61.0	533	45.3	134	42.7	667	44.8	4.0
	Thous.	%	Thous.	%	Thous.	%	Thous.	%	%
Employed***	1,462.6	100.0	115.7	100.0	50.7	100.0	166.4	100.0	11.3
Agriculture	86.1	5.9	33.1	28.6	8.6	16.9	41.7	25.0	48.4
Industry	353.2	24.2	18.2	15.7	9.0	17.8	27.2	16.3	7.7
Construction	107.1	7.3	14.7	12.7	4.2	8.2	18.9	11.4	17.6
Services	916.2	62.6	49.7	43.0	28.9	57.1	78.3	47.3	8.6
	$	%	$	%	$	%	$	%	%
GDP/Employed	18,840	100.0	10,170	100.0	6,190	100.0	8,960	100.0	47.6
Agriculture	19,200	101.9	11,660	114.7	8,020	129.6	10,910	121.8	56.8
Industry	19,500	103.5	5,050	49.7	4,550	73.5	4,890	54.6	25.1
Construction	20,580	109.2	11,290	111.0	16,660	269.1	12,490	139.4	60.7
Services	18,350	97.4	10,720	105.4	4,640	75.0	8,490	94.8	46.3

* Statistical Abstract of Israel, 1987 and Administered Territories Quarterly, November 1987
** At factor costs for the West Bank and Gaza Strip and for Israel in market prices, both at exchange rate of NIS 1.49 = $1
*** Includes 94,700 workers from WB/GS employed in Israel

4.2 Employment and Productivity

In 1968, the number of workers in construction in the West Bank had dropped to 8,500 (from 22,000 in 1965) while the number in the Gaza Strip had remained relatively constant at 4,400. In addition, there were another 4,100 workers from the Territories in Israel employed in construction. Thus the total number employed in construction was some 17,000 out of a total employment of 110,000 (15.5 per cent)[11].

In 1968, the 12,900 employed in the West Bank and Gaza generated a building area of 85,300 sq. m. This represents an area of building of 6.6 sq. m. per worker (8.6 in the West Bank and 2.8 in Gaza). In Israel, the building area per worker in 1968 reached 44.5 sq.m. or 6.7 times the level in the WB/GS (see Table 4.2.1).

The table (4.2.1) shows employment, building area and area built per worker for seven separate years over three-year intervals, from 1968 to 1986. Since building area construction activity represents on average over 90 per cent of construction activities in the WB/GS and nearly 80 per cent in Israel, we will use this figure (divided by total construction employment) as an indicator of productivity in building.

Note that, by 1974 in the WB/GS, although the labor force in construction had dropped by over 25 per cent, building area had risen over sevenfold reaching a level of nearly 10 times the area built per worker in 1968. While this level was one-quarter higher than in Israel, Israel had a higher proportion of the work-force engaged in non-housing construction activities so this should be compensated for. Note also, in Israel, that the drop in construction after 1974 was not accompanied by a similar drop in employment. In the WB/GS, while unpaid and unrecorded family labor is extensively utilized, this is not reflected in official statistics.

In 1980, the total building area in the WB/GS reached 1,078,000 sq. m. with a work force of 13,200. Thus the area built per worker was 81.7 sq.m. as compared with 43.9 sq.m. in Israel. Thus, productivity was officially 86 per cent higher in the Territories.

By 1986, there were 18,900 workers in the Territories constructing 1,234,000 sq.m. for an area built per worker of

65.3 sq.m. Note that in 1986 as compared with 1980, productivity declined both in the Territories and in Israel – 65.3 and 38.8 sq.m. respectively. The output per worker in Israel was even lower than in 1968 but this is probably due to the fact that output declined at a faster rate than employment.

Production methods in the West Bank and Gaza are still simple and labor-intensive and much less industrialized or mechanized than those in Israel. "Early Israeli attempts to introduce more capital intensive methods (e.g. poured concrete techniques) met with strong resistance. Such Israeli methods, while cheaper and less labor-intensive, could not faithfully produce the traditional West Bank stone and cement dwelling and were, therefore, resisted."[12]

An indicator of non-industrialized methods is the fact that while over 40 per cent of the cement used in Israel is in bulk form (i.e. mechanized), only around 6 per cent is in bulk form[13] in the territories. The percentage in Israel would have been even higher except for the existence of "cheap" labor which prevents modernization. It is quite likely that much of the private building in the WB/GS uses unpaid family labor which is not reflected in labor statistics.

Considering that over 42 per cent of the labor in Israeli construction is from the WB/GS and another 16 per cent is Israeli Arab labor, then nearly 65 per cent of Israeli construction labor is ethnic Arab (see Table 4.2.2). If one makes allowances for the predominance of Jews in non-direct and non-production tasks, then manual labor in this branch is overwhelmingly ethnic Arab. Nevertheless, even when all allowances are made it is difficult to account for the lower productivity in Israel as compared with the WB/GS.

Forty-eight per cent of labor from the Territories in Israel is employed in construction as compared with just over 11 per cent so employed in the Territories. Nearly one-quarter of WB/GS labor is employed in construction whether in Israel or in the Territories. Nearly 71 per cent of this construction labor is employed in Israel. While over 42 per cent of Israel's construction labor is from the Territories, only 6 per cent of her total labor force is from there.

Employment in construction, whether in Israel or the WB/GS area, has been considerable, especially since 1974. Table 4.2.3 shows the development of construction labor and total labor between 1970 and 1986 for the West Bank and Gaza. The same data is presented in percentage form in Table 4.2.4. Total construction labor in the West Bank and Gaza which involved 12,800 workers in 1970 (8.4 per cent of the total) dropped to 8,500 by 1972. From then until 1986, it rose gradually at 5.9 per cent per annum to reach 18,900. This is still lower than the period immediately preceding the occupation but it reflects a continuing rise in output and productivity (as a percentage of total). After an initial drop from 8.4 per cent to 6.2 per cent between 1970 and 1972, local construction labor as a percentage of total local WB/GS labor rose gradually to reach 11.4 per cent in 1986.

WB/GS labor in Israel rose very rapidly after 1970 and construction labor rose steadily between 1970 (11,200) and 1983 (44,300) at a per annum rate of 11.2 per cent. Between 1983 and 1986, it remained at a steady level. As Table 4.2.4 shows, WB/GS construction labor in Israel as a percentage of total WB/GS labor in Israel remained at around half between 1970 and 1986.

The total number in construction, whether in Israel or the WB/GS, rose from 24,000 in 1970 and reached 64,400 in 1986, a per annum growth rate of 6.4 per cent. In percentage terms, construction labor rose from 13.8 per cent of the total in 1970 to 24.9 per cent in 1981, and has remained at about one-quarter since then.

Most (about 97 per cent) of the West Bank and Gaza employed persons working in Israel were and still are employees, working for daily wages. An even higher percentage of construction workers are employees (see Table 4.2.5). The daily wages for employees, construction and total, are shown for the period 1970 to 1986 in Table 4.2.6. Notice that the wages for employees working in Israel, while originally (1970) significantly lower in the West Bank and Gaza, have remained lower until 1986. In general, the West Bank and Gaza employees earned less than this average so there has always been a wage advantage in Israel. In most (but not all) years there is a wage advantage for workers from the West Bank over Gaza. Furthermore, workers in construction earn on average 10 per cent more than the average (total) wage.

Table 4.2.7 shows, in monthly terms, the average wages of

West Bank employees (construction and total) in Israel and compares them with average Israeli wages. This will be discussed shortly. Separate data for Israeli wages in construction excluding WB/GS employees, were not available but for 1986 it was deduced that the NIS 894 average monthly wage in construction really consisted of NIS 511 for WB/GS employees and NIS 1,410 for Israeli employees. Therefore the WB/GS wage was only 36 per cent of those

Table 4.2.1

Construction Employment, Building Area & Productivity in the West Bank, Gaza and Israel – 1968-1986 (Thousands)

Year	1968	1971	1974	1977	1980	1983	1986**
Employed (thousands)							
West Bank	8.5	5.6	7.4	9.6	9.7	10.9	14.7
Gaza Strip	4.4	2.4	2.1	3.3	3.5	3.7	4.2
WB + GS	12.9	8.0	9.5	12.9	13.2	14.6	18.9
Israel Including WB/GS Labor	77.0	106.0	128.7	114.3	114.8	131.3	107.2
WB/GS Labor in Israel	4.1	17.7	35.5	28.5	35.6	44.2	45.4
Total WB/GS Construction Labor	17.0	25.7	45.0	41.4	48.8	58.8	64.3
Building Area (thousand M²)*							
West Bank	72.9	194.9	470.1	655.2	753.0	709.4	941.3
Gaza Strip	12.4	28.2	133.9	252.2	325.0	329.0	292.8
WB + GS	85.3	223.1	604.0	907.4	1078.0	1038.4	1234.1
Israel	3423.0	6170.0	6433.0	5290.0	5035.0	4855.0	4160.0
Productivity (M²) Area Built per Worker							
West Bank	8.6	34.8	63.5	68.2	77.6	65.1	64.0
Gaza Strip	2.8	11.8	63.8	76.4	92.8	88.9	69.7
WB + GS	6.6	27.9	63.6	70.3	81.7	77.1	65.3
Israel	44.5	58.2	50.0	46.3	43.9	37.0	38.8
WB + GS as % of Israel	14.8	47.9	127.2	151.8	186.1	208.4	168.3

Source: Statistical Abstract(s) of Israel
* Building Area is based on average of building starts and completions
** 1986 – updated CBS data published by the Ministry of Construction and Housing

Table 4.2.2

1986 WB/GS and Israel Sectorial and Ethnic Employment
(No. = Thousands)[1]

	Agriculture No.	%	Industry[3] No.	%	Construction No.	%	Services[4] No.	%	Total No.	%
West Bank/Gaza Strip										
1. WB/GS Arabs Employed in WB/GS	41.6	25.1	27.2	16.3	18.9	11.3	78.6	47.2	166.3	100.0
2. WB/GS Arabs Employed in Israel	14.9	15.8	16.5	17.5	45.4	48.0	17.7	18.7	94.5	100.0
3. Total WB/GS Employment (1+2)	56.5	21.7	43.7	16.7	64.3	24.7	96.3	36.9	260.8	100.0
4. Percentage of WB/GS Labor Employed in Israel (2/3)	–	26.4	–	37.8	–	70.6	–	18.4	–	36.2
5. Percentage of Israel's Labor from WB/GS (2/10)	–	17.6	–	4.7	–	42.4	–	1.9	–	6.5
Israel[2]										
6. Jewish Labor in Israel	57.4	12.9	296.3	24.4	38.2	3.1	824.4	67.8	1216.3	100.0
7. Israeli Arab Labor in Isr.	12.6	8.3	38.5	25.4	23.6	15.6	76.9	50.7	151.6	100.0
8. Total Israeli Labor in Israel (6+7)	70.0	5.1	334.8	24.5	61.8	4.5	901.3	65.9	1367.9	100.0
9. Arab Labor in Israel (2+7)	27.5	11.2	55.0	22.3	69.0	28.0	94.6	38.4	246.1	100.0
10. Total Employment in Israel(6+9)	84.9	5.8	351.3	24.0	107.2	7.3	919.0	62.8	1462.4	100.0
11. Arab Labor in Israel or Percentage of Labor in Israel (9/10)	–	32.4	–	15.7	–	64.4	–	10.3	–	16.8

1. Source: Statistical Abstract of Israel, Jerusalem 1987
2. Jewish Labor in WB/GS is only included in data on Israel
3. Industry includes manufacturing, handicrafts, electricity and mining
4. Services include all categories not covered elsewhere, both public and private.

Table 4.2.3

WB/GS Residents Employed in WB/GS & Israel in Construction
(Thousands)

Year	West Bank Total	West Bank Constr.	Gaza Strip Total	Gaza Strip Constr.	WB/GS Total	WB/GS Constr.	Israel Total	Israel Constr.	WB/GS + Israel Total	WB/GS + Israel Constr.
1970	99.8	8.4	52.9	4.5	152.7	12.8	20.6	11.2	173.3	24.0
1972	90.3	6.5	46.0	1.9	136.3	8.5	52.4	25.9	188.7	34.4
1974	95.0	6.7	46.7	1.9	141.7	8.8	68.7	36.1	210.4	44.9
1976	92.6	9.3	48.3	2.2	140.9	11.6	64.9	32.6	205.8	44.2
1978	94.0	10.2	48.7	3.4	142.7	13.6	68.2	30.6	210.9	44.2
1980	94.3	10.1	46.3	3.4	140.6	13.5	75.1	35.6	215.7	49.1
1981	93.5	11.1	46.6	3.9	140.1	15.0	75.8	38.7	215.9	53.7
1982	97.5	10.3	46.1	3.9	143.6	14.2	79.1	44.8	222.7	56.0
1983	99.1	10.9	45.6	3.7	144.7	14.6	87.8	44.3	232.5	58.9
1984	104.0	11.8	47.0	4.0	151.0	15.8	90.3	43.6	241.3	59.4
1985	103.8	12.9	48.9	4.1	152.7	17.0	89.2	42.5	241.9	59.5
1986	115.7	14.7	50.7	4.2	166.4	18.9	94.7	45.5	261.1	64.4

Source: Statistical Abstract(s) of Israel

Table 4.2.4

WB/GS Residents Employed in WB/GS & Israel in Construction (%)

Year	WEST BANK		GAZA STRIP		WB/GS		ISRAEL		WB/GS+ISRAEL		
	% of Total	% C/T	% of Total	% Constr.	% of Total	% Constr.	% of Total	% Constr.	% of Total	% of Cons.	% C/T
	% of Total	Constr.	% C/T	% of Total Constr.	% C/T	% of Total Constr.	% C/T	% of Total Constr.	% C/T	% of Total	% of Cons.	% C/T
1970	57.6	35.0	8.4	30.5	18.7	8.5	88.1	53.3	8.4	11.9	46.7	54.3	100.0	100.0	13.8
1972	47.8	18.9	7.2	24.4	5.5	4.1	72.2	24.7	6.2	27.8	75.3	49.5	100.0	100.0	18.2
1974	45.1	14.9	7.1	22.2	4.7	4.1	67.3	19.6	6.2	32.7	80.4	52.5	100.0	100.0	21.3
1976	45.0	21.0	10.0	23.5	5.0	4.6	68.5	26.2	8.2	31.5	73.8	50.3	100.0	100.0	21.5
1978	44.6	23.1	10.8	23.1	7.7	7.0	67.7	30.8	9.5	32.3	69.2	44.8	100.0	100.0	21.0
1980	43.7	20.6	10.7	21.5	6.9	7.3	65.2	27.5	9.6	34.8	72.5	47.4	100.0	100.0	22.8
1981	43.3	20.7	11.9	21.6	7.3	8.4	64.9	27.9	10.7	35.1	72.1	51.0	100.0	100.0	24.9
1982	43.8	18.4	10.6	20.7	7.0	8.5	64.5	25.4	9.9	35.5	74.6	52.8	100.0	100.0	25.1
1983	42.6	18.5	11.0	19.6	6.3	8.2	62.2	24.8	10.1	37.8	75.2	50.4	100.0	100.0	25.3
1984	43.1	19.9	11.3	19.5	6.7	8.5	62.6	26.6	10.4	37.4	73.4	48.3	100.0	100.0	24.6
1985	42.9	21.7	12.4	20.2	6.9	8.4	63.1	28.6	11.1	36.9	71.4	47.6	100.0	100.0	24.6
1986	44.3	22.8	12.7	19.4	6.5	8.2	63.7	29.3	11.4	36.3	70.7	48.0	100.0	100.0	24.7

Source: Statistical Abstract(s) of Israel

Table 4.2.5

WB/GS Employees Working in Israel
(Thousands)

Year	Employed Persons		Employees		% of Employed		% Construction of Total
	Total	Construction	Total	Construction	Total	Construction	
1970	20.6	11.2	19.8	10.8	96.1	96.4	54.5
1972	52.4	25.9	50.8	25.3	96.9	97.7	49.8
1975	66.3	36.1	63.9	35.2	96.4	97.5	55.1
1978	68.2	30.6	67.4	30.6	98.8	100.0	45.4
1980	75.1	35.6	73.2	35.1	97.5	98.6	48.0
1981	75.8	38.7	73.9	38.2	97.5	98.7	51.7
1982	79.1	41.8	76.6	40.9	96.8	97.8	53.4
1983	87.8	44.3	84.3	43.3	96.0	97.7	51.4
1984	90.3	43.6	86.9	42.8	96.2	98.2	49.3
1985	89.2	42.5	86.1	41.4	96.5	97.4	48.1
1986	94.7	45.5	91.6	44.4	96.7	97.6	48.5

Source: Statistical Abstract(s) of Israel

Table 4.2.6

Average Daily Wages of WB/GS Employees

| Year | Working in Israel | | | | Working in WB/GS + Israel | | | |
| | Construction | | Total | | Construction | | Total | |
	WB	GS	WB	GS	WB	GS	WB	GS
In IL								
1970	13.0	12.5	11.8	11.7	10.3	7.0	7.9	6.5
1972	19.0	19.5	17.0	17.6	18.2	17.3	13.7	12.8
1975	48.4	45.4	44.6	41.9	47.2	44.6	39.6	38.7
1978	120.8	120.0	112.1	109.2	120.2	118.2	105.5	102.9
In NIS								
1980	0.043	0.047	0.039	0.042	0.043	0.046	0.036	0.039
1981	0.125	0.115	0.112	0.104	0.122	0.113	0.104	0.102
1982	0.271	0.268	0.248	0.247	0.266	0.262	0.231	0.242
1983	0.662	0.642	0.606	0.599	0.656	0.631	0.566	0.593
1984	2.606	2.502	2.420	2.284	2.664	2.485	2.533	2.527
1985	10.84	9.96	10.04	9.08	10.81	9.81	10.11	9.57
1986	19.60	20.18	18.18	18.43	19.10	19.83	17.28	17.95

Source: Statistical Abstract(s) of Israel

from Israel. This excludes consideration of National Insurance and other benefits. The table shows that average WB/GS wages in recent years are around 42 per cent of those in Israel and in construction about 45 per cent. However, it should be noted that Israeli wages for Israelis in construction are above average wages so that WB/GS wages in construction are probably only 36 per cent of Israeli construction wages. Nevertheless, the construction sector is the most highly paid sector from the WB/GS.

Wages earned by (official) WB/GS workers in Israel are subject to deductions for tax and National Insurance. In 1986, official employees represented 41,800 out of the 91,600 total employees (a minority of these others also had tax and National Insurance deductions made). These deductions are governed by tax law and National Insurance legislation and may account for 30 per cent of earnings. A large proportion of WB/GS employees working in Israel pay their share of the National Insurance scheme, yet they are not entitled to benefits accrued on the basis of residency such

Table 4.2.7

Monthly Wages of WB/GS Employees in Israel And a Comparison with Average Israeli Wages

	Average Wages in Israel WB/GS Employees		Israel	WB/GS Wages as % of Average Israel Wages	
	Total	Construction	Total	Total	Construction
In IL					
1970	256	282	688	37.2	41.0
1972	381	423	912	41.8	46.4
1975	981	1,069	2,205	44.5	48.5
1978	2,743	2,982	6,693	41.0	44.5
In NIS					
1980	1.23	1.33	2.90	42.4	45.9
1981	2.92	3.16	6.90	42.3	45.8
1982	6.57	7.10	15.00	43.8	47.0
1983	16.90	18.30	38.40	44.0	47.7
1984	76.70	83.20	186.00	41.2	44.7
1985	256.00	279.00	662.00	38.6	42.2
1986	471.00	511.00	1,092.00	43.1	46.7

Source: Statistical Abstract(s) of Israel

as old-age and survivors benefits, disability benefits, unemployment benefits and children's allowances. The latter was partially compensated for in the form of a special allowance for the first two children. Since 1980, pension payments have been paid to the few construction workers who had completed 10 years of service and had reached retirement age. Other benefits such as sickness leave, dismissal compensation and wife and clothing allowances are not paid[14]. Officially, the difference between the taxes and insurance collected and benefits paid out is allocated to the budget of the "Civil Administration" (military government).

4.3 Housing

Initially, with the occupation of the Territories in 1967, there was a degree of dislocation, and only after 1970 (see Table 4.3.1) did the building area reach the pre-war magnitude. In 1968, it was less than half the 1966 area. Nevertheless, the per annum rate of growth for the period 1968 to 1979 for the average starts and completions area (see Table 4.3.1) was 26.3 percent. In contrast, the rate for 1979 to 1986 was only 1.5 per cent per annum, even less than the population growth. In the West Bank, residential starts for 1968 to 1979 increased from 51,000 sq.m. to 655,700 sq.m., a per annum rate of 26.1 per cent; while in the Gaza Strip residential starts increased from a very low 3,800 sq. m. in 1968 to 342,500 sq. m. in 1979, a per annum growth rate of 50.6 per cent.

This is a quite unprecedented rate of growth. The respective per annum rates of growth in residential starts from 1979 to 1986 was 3.4 per cent and -4.5 percent. Notice the negative growth rate in the Gaza Strip after 1979.

One of the reasons for the high growth rate from 1968 was that construction activity had dropped sharply in the period immediately after the war. It recovered and increased fairly rapidly until relative stagnation set in after 1979 which lasted until the present.

If one looks at new 1987 data for residential building starts, then there is an actual decrease from 1979 – 971,400 vs. 999,800 sq. m. (and 1,057,200 in 1986). Just when the WB/GS population growth rate (in the 1980s) has accelerated, housing starts have declined.

The construction contribution to the GDP has jumped to over 14 per cent in the West Bank in 1986 and to over 22 per cent in Gaza (see Table 4.3.1), a WB/GS average of nearly 16 per cent. Domestic construction employment in 1986 reached nearly 13 per cent in the West Bank and over 8 per cent in Gaza, a WB/GS average of over 11 per cent. The productivity or GDP per employed person in construction as compared with average GDP per employed person in all sectors was 111 per cent in the West Bank, 269 per cent in the Gaza Strip and 139 per cent average for the two territories. The difference between construction's share in domestic output and employment may be explained by relatively high labor productivity in this sector and by unpaid family labor working on week-end vacation from employment in Israel.

After an initial (1968) low proportion of residential building starts, especially in Gaza, with around 18 per cent of total starts (but with 83 per cent of completions), building activity was over 80 per cent residential in the West Bank and over 85 per cent residential in the Gaza Strip.

"The concentration on housing came in part as a result of increased demand for dwellings generated by the rise in population incomes. The Arab inhabitants of the areas are culturally predisposed toward investments in home ownership. Other factors responsible for the expansion of residential construction include the lack of alternative investment opportunities, an unwillingness to invest in other branches of the economy because of the prevailing uncertainties associated with the occupation of the Territories, and the people's determination to assert their rights to the land in the face of continuous threats of confiscation."[15]

In the early years of occupation (e.g. before 1979), total investment in the Territories averaged well over one-third of the GDP but since then it has dropped to between 25 per cent and 30 per cent (see Table 4.3.2). In the earlier years the proportion of investment in building and construction works of total fixed capital investment exceeded three quarters, but more recently it has been averaging around two-thirds. Taking non-residential building and public works into account, then around an estimated three-quarters of this is in housing. Investment in construction in fixed 1980 prices after reaching a high in 1979 declined until 1986 when it finally exceeded the 1979 figure by 7 per cent.

While in 1968 public building starts reached 17.7 per cent of total building starts in the Territories, for residential building this was only one per cent. In the West Bank, in 1968, due to the residual from previous public building under the Jordanian regime, nearly 60 per cent of building completions came from the public building sector (see Table 4.3.3). Over three-quarters (76.5 per cent) of the public building was residential.

By 1974, public building starts in the Territories had been reduced to 2 per cent of total building and 0.8 per cent of housing, and by 1978, public residential building had virtually ceased – 1,000 sq.m. starts and 3,000 finishes. Since 1979, there has been no public housing construction although loans were available in Gaza for resettling of refugees.

In Gaza in 1968, there was practically no public residential building despite the refugee status of the majority of the population. By the mid-70s, the only serious attempt to resettle refugees took place in Gaza. These government-sponsored but mostly privately-built projects involved refugees who were willing and financially able to leave their camp homes. The units were located on land leased from the government for 99 years. Although in a minority of the cases the government built the units, in all cases the refugees assumed full infrastructure costs and all costs of construction. The participants are required to demolish their camp homes for which they receive a nominal payment. Some refugees qualified for certain housing-loan schemes of the Israeli administration. By the end of 1985, over 37,000 individuals, representing less than 10 per cent of the refugees, had occupied nearly 5,000 housing units. Of these, less than one-sixth were built in the framework of public housing, and these were completed prior to 1979[16]. The Benvenisti and Khayat Atlas notes 6,382 plots allocated for the "build-your-own project" in 1986.

In the West Bank, 3,990 families received around JD 27m. (over $80m.) from the Jordanian-Palestinian Joint Committee for Housing. This involved an average of nearly $20,000 per family between the years 1979 and 1985. Except for this loan scheme, the burden of residential construction has fallen entirely on private individuals[17]. While the Jordanian Five Year Plan (1986-1990) had made provision for housing loans and investment, little was actually done by mid-1988 when the Jordanian government broke official links with the West Bank.

The annual number of new dwellings in the Territories (6,971 units) actually declined between 1976 (the earliest year for statistics) and 1986 (6,538 units) as can be seen in Table 4.3.4. The average per annum decline was 0.6 per cent. It should be noted however, that the average size of new dwelling was only 85 sq.m. in 1976 as compared with 130 sq. m. in 1987 – an average growth rate of 4.2 per annum. This resulted in a growth rate in area of dwellings (excludes communal area of buildings, i.e. net) of 3.6 per cent per annum since 1976. Note, however, that there was practically no growth in total area completed since 1982. The total number of rooms completed each year since 1976 increased from 21,252 to 25,009 in 1986 – an annual rate of increase of 1.6 per cent. The average number of rooms per new dwelling increased from 2.9 to 3.7, an annual rate of increase of 2.5 per cent.

Gaza development lagged behind that of the West Bank. Their number of dwellings decreased from 2,198 in 1976 to 1,402 (a negative rate of -4.4 per cent per annum). Their number of rooms remained the same at the end of the decade (5,900), although it exceeded 6,000 in 1982. Their area of dwellings declined from 1979 although the average area per dwelling in Gaza nearly doubled – from 74.7 to 144.5 sq.m., an increase of 6.8 per cent per annum. During the decade, despite the stagnation in building, especially as a measure of the number of dwellings, the number of households increased at a rate of over 2.7 per cent per annum.

A recent survey[18] reports that in Arab East Jerusalem, during the years 1977 to 1984, 43,000 sq.m. were built annually of which some 85 per cent or 36,500 sq.m., were for housing. On a per capita basis this is 0.4 m^2 per annum of which 0.34 m^2 is for housing, as compared to 1.3 m^2 and 0.9 m^2 for the Jewish sectors of Jerusalem. In terms of number of housing unit per 1,000 population: for Arabs, this was 1.9 per annum, as against 9.0 for Jews for the comparable

Table 4.3.1

WB/GS Area of Building by Initiating Sector and Purpose
(In Thousands of Square Meters)

	1968	1970	1972	1974	1976	1978	1979	1980	1981	1982	1983	1984	1985	1986*
Buildings Begun –														
Total WB/GS	87.9	146.5	499.5	692.3	944.5	1119.5	1209.6	1145.6	1205.7	1022.2	1008.1	989.5	1082.2	1317.1
West Bank – Total	66.8	129.1	325.5	557.7	646.7	786.4	797.6	756.3	805.5	750.4	669.9	677.2	775.6	1032.5
Residential	51.0	95.3	259.7	452.3	529.8	638.2	655.7	631.9	661.6	659.9	567.4	546.3	647.2	830.8
Gaza Strip – Total	21.1	16.6	124.0	134.6	297.8	333.1	412.0	389.3	400.2	271.8	338.2	312.3	306.6	284.6
Residential	3.8	11.8	106.1	124.3	243.9	276.4	342.5	327.0	340.3	237.2	292.5	277.2	263.0	248.0
Total WB/GS Residential	54.8	107.1	365.8	549.6	773.7	914.6	998.2	958.9	1001.9	897.1	859.9	823.5	910.2	1078.8
Building Completed														
Total WB/GS	82.6	114.2	290.4	515.7	802.0	912.7	1019.5	1010.3	1029.4	1048.7	1068.7	983.1	1005.5	1151.2
West Bank – Total	79.0	101.7	199.0	382.5	580.4	655.3	718.1	749.7	716.7	686.1	748.8	695.1	777.6	857.8
Residential	63.3	71.2	159.8	320.8	473.5	542.5	571.7	624.7	599.6	586.0	630.0	579.8	654.8	708.6
Gaza Strip – Total	3.6	12.5	91.4	133.2	221.6	257.4	294.9	260.6	312.7	362.6	319.9	288.0	227.9	293.4
Residential	3.0	8.7	74.9	126.2	193.0	210.1	248.1	217.9	258.6	305.0	274.3	246.0	196.1	257.0
Total WB/GS Residential	66.3	79.9	234.7	447.0	666.5	752.6	819.8	842.6	858.2	891.0	904.3	825.8	850.9	965.6
Total WB/GS Average Area (1/2 Starts + Completions)	85.2	130.4	395.0	604.0	873.2	1016.1	1114.6	1078.0	1117.6	1035.4	1038.4	986.4	1043.8	1234.1

Source: Statistical Abstract(s) of Israel

* 1986 Data adjusted by updated Ministry of Construction and Housing data

Table 4.3.2

Analysis of Gross Domestic Capital Formations, 1979-1986
(NIS Thousand at 1980 Prices)

	GDP	Total Investment GDCF	Fixed Capital Investment	Inv.in Building & Construction Works	GDCF: by GDP	Build & Const. as % of Fixed Investment
1979	3,256	871	1,088	784	26.8	72.1
1980	4,098	1,376	1,014	756	33.6	74.6
1981	3,675	950	964	704	25.9	73.0
1982	4,128	1,156	1,075	726	28.0	67.5
1983	3,979	1,044	1,036	664	26.2	64.1
1984	4,229	1,018	1,012	640	24.1	63.0
1985	4,158	1,128	1,104	736	27.1	66.7
1986	5,061	1,455	1,307	843	28.7	64.5

Source: Statistical Abstract(s) of Israel

Table 4.3.3

Private and Public Building in the WB/GS
(Thousand Square Meters)

Year	Total Building		Public Building		Private Building	
	Total	Residential	Total	Residential	Total	Residential
Starts						
1968	87.8	54.8	15.5	0.6	72.4	54.2
1970	146.5	107.1	–	–	–	–
1972	499.5	365.8	–	–	–	–
1974	692.3	576.6	13.7	4.8	678.6	571.8
1975	827.3	693.7	66.8	51.6	760.5	642.1
1976	940.9	773.7	19.5	8.0	921.4	765.7
1978	1119.5	914.6	11.2	1.0	1108.3	913.6
1980	1145.6	958.9	10.8	–	1134.8	958.9
1982	1031.7	902.6	5.8	–	1025.9	902.6
1984	992.8	823.2	4.6	–	988.2	823.2
1985	1089.7	911.3	16.0	–	1073.7	911.3
1986	1317.1	1057.2	22.9	–	1294.2	1057.2
1987	1286.2	971.9	14.9	–	1238.4	924.4
Completions						
1968	82.3	66.3	47.5	36.1	35.1	30.2
1970	114.2	79.9	–	–	–	–
1972	290.4	234.7	–	–	–	–
1974	515.7	447.0	23.7	13.9	492.0	433.1
1975	611.5	504.5	23.1	9.0	588.4	495.5
1976	802.0	666.5	58.3	44.7	743.7	621.8
1978	912.7	752.6	15.9	3.0	896.8	749.6
1980	1010.3	842.6	4.7	–	1005.6	842.6
1982	1072.1	903.1	8.8	–	1063.2	903.1
1984	986.3	826.7	8.2	–	978.1	826.7
1985	1010.9	851.5	9.0	–	1001.9	851.5
1986	1151.2	947.7	20.3	–	1131.0	947.7
1987	1169.4	968.4	15.3	–	1154.1	968.4

Source: Ministry of Construction and Housing, and the Central Bureau of Statistics

period. The average per annum role of Arab building in Jerusalem was lower than in the West Bank where this was 0.9 m^2 per capita and 6 per 1,000 people. The survey argues that this indicates that many East Jerusalem Arabs are leaving the city limits to live in suburbs and nearby towns and villages, and that there is a large increase in urban density in areas surrounding Jerusalem. Nevertheless, the WBDP reports that Arab population of East Jerusalem has grown by 98 per cent between 1967 and 1987.

Table 4.3.4

1976-86 WB/GS Dwellings & Their Total Area, Average Area and Rooms in Newly Completed Buildings

		Dwelling - No. of Units	No. of Rooms	Areas of Dwellings (1,000 M^2)	Average Rooms in Dwelling*	Average Area per Dwelling (M^2)
1976	WB	4,773	15,356	428.9	3.0	89.9
	GS	2,198	5,896	164.2	2.0	74.7
	Total	6,971	21,252	593.1	2.9	85.1
1977	WB	4,498	15,441	469.9	3.1	104.5
	GS	1,373	5,123	173.2	3.6	126.1
	Total	5,871	20,564	643.1	3.2	109.5
1978	WB	4,581	16,602	496.0	3.3	108.3
	GS	1,559	5,680	194.6	3.5	124.8
	Total	6,140	22,282	690.6	3.4	112.5
1979	WB	4,746	16,735	537.6	3.3	113.3
	GS	1,759	6,530	233.2	3.7	132.6
	Total	6,505	23,508	770.8	3.4	118.5
1980	WB	5,057	17,978	589.0	3.3	116.5
	GS	1,577	5,815	204.5	3.6	129.7
	Total	6,634	23,793	793.5	3.4	119.6
1981	WB	4,451	16,461	534.3	3.5	120.0
	GS	1,784	6,565	238.4	3.7	133.6
	Total	6,235	23,026	772.7	3.6	123.9
1982	WB	4,293	15,991	559.1	3.6	130.2
	GS	2,116	8,130	275.6	3.8	130.2
	Total	6,409	24,121	834.7	3.7	130.2
1983	WB	4,472	16,654	600.4	3.6	134.3
	GS	1,802	7,058	239.0	3.9	132.6
	Total	6,274	23,712	839.4	3.7	133.8
1984	WB	4,223	16,123	534.8	3.6	126.6
	GS	1,597	6,432	214.4	4.0	134.3
	Total	5,820	22,555	749.2	3.7	128.7
1985	WB	4,514	17,680	594.7	3.7	131.7
	GS	1,223	5,040	168.6	4.1	137.9
	Total	5,737	22,720	763.3	3.8	133.0
1986	WB	5,136	19,084	643.0	3.5	125.2
	GS	1,402	5,925	202.6	4.2	144.5
	Total	6,538	25,009	845.6	3.7	129.3
WB/GS Per Annum Growth Rate		-0.6	1.6	3.6	2.5	4.3

Source: Statistical Abstract(s) of Israel
* Average rooms excludes additional rooms to existing dwellings

To sum up this section: the main features are the still heavy expenditures on construction – but at an ever-declining rate. Investment is mainly in construction; construction is mainly for housing; and housing construction is mainly private. Since 1979 there has been a significant slowdown. This is even more pronounced in the Gaza Strip. Nevertheless, in recent years there has been an improvement in the ownership of household facilities since 1974.

In the preceding discussion nearly all the data has been based on information released by the CBS. Based on the author's construction experience it may be that many unofficial residential units are being constructed but not recorded. In that case, building data might have to be adjusted upwards.

In section 4.6 we shall discuss objective housing conditions.

4.4 Non-Residential Construction

While, in Israel, construction of non-residential buildings (hotels, commercial and office buildings, industrial, public, social, and non-residential farm buildings) accounts for over 28 per cent on average of total building (measured in sq.m.), in the West Bank and Gaza this barely reaches 17 per cent (see Table 4.3.3). While in earlier years, especially in 1968, public building accounted for around half of the activity in the West Bank and Gaza (the residual of public building from the Egyptian and Jordanian occupations), by the mid-70s (see Table 4.4.1) this accounted for only around 6-8 per cent; and in the 1980s this dropped to around 2-3 per cent – all of it in Gaza.

In the West Bank, non-residential building (an indicator of economic and social development) did not exceed 20 per cent (average of starts and completions) since 1972 and in Gaza since 1970.

Furthermore, in the West Bank since 1981, all the building has been private with no public-funded building taking place. This means in effect that only a small amount of the total non-residential building is for social or public purposes, especially as compared with Israel. Even in the Gaza Strip a residual of publicly-funded building is taking place which averaged around 10 per cent of the total and reached nearly 19 per cent in 1986.

These statistics (from Table 4.4.1) do not include construction of public works and other civil engineering projects (not measured by area) such as pipelines, roads, bridges, waterworks, power plants, etc., intended mainly for the Arab inhabitants. Many of the non-residential building projects are intended for the Israeli military and/or

Table 4.4.1

Non-Residential Building in the WB/GS
(Thousand Square Meters)

	WEST BANK			GAZA STRIP			WB/GS TOTAL		
	Total NR	% NR*	% Private	Total NR	% NR	% Priv.	Total NR	% NR	% Priv
Starts									
1968	15.8	23.7	32.3	17.3	82.0	75.7	33.1	37.7	55.0
1970	33.8	26.2	–	5.8	34.9	–	39.6	27.2	–
1972	65.8	20.2	–	17.9	14.4	–	83.7	18.6	–
1974	105.4	18.9	–	10.3	7.7	–	115.7	16.7	92.3
1976	116.9	18.1	93.2	53.9	18.1	93.3	170.8	18.1	93.3
1978	148.2	18.8	96.1	56.7	17.0	92.2	204.9	18.3	95.0
1979	131.9	17.6	95.8	69.5	16.6	90.2	201.4	17.2	92.4
1980	124.4	16.4	96.9	62.3	16.00	88.9	186.7	16.3	92.0
1981	142.7	17.9	–	59.3	14.8	–	202.0	17.1	96.5
1982	91.6	12.2	100.0	35.0	12.8	96.7	103.2	12.4	98.9
1983	102.5	15.3	100.0	45.7	13.5	80.5	148.2	14.7	94.0
1984	130.9	19.3	100.0	35.0	11.2	96.9	165.9	16.8	99.3
1985	128.4	16.6	100.0	43.6	14.2	86.0	172.0	15.9	96.5
1986	189.5	19.5	100.0	37.7	13.9	90.2	227.2	18.3	98.4
Completions									
1968	15.7	19.9	29.3	0.6	16.7	50.0	16.3	19.7	30.1
1970	30.5	30.0	–	3.8	30.4	–	34.3	27.1	–
1972	39.2	19.7	–	16.5	18.1	–	55.7	19.2	–
1974	61.7	16.1	–	7.0	5.3	–	68.7	13.3	85.7
1976	106.9	18.4	88.3	28.6	12.9	96.2	135.5	16.9	90.0
1978	112.8	17.2	94.8	47.3	18.3	85.2	160.1	17.5	91.9
1979	246.4	19.9	–	46.8	15.8	89.7	293.2	18.7	95.3
1980	125.0	14.3	97.1	42.7	16.40	97.4	167.7	14.8	97.2
1981	111.9	15.6	–	54.2	17.3	–	166.1	16.8	99.2
1982	108.3	15.3	100.0	57.6	15.9	94.8	165.9	15.5	98.2
1983	118.8	15.9	100.0	45.6	14.3	93.6	164.4	15.4	98.2
1984	115.3	16.6	100.0	42.0	14.6	91.2	157.3	16.0	97.6
1985	122.8	15.8	100.0	31.8	14.0	91.2	154.6	15.4	98.2
1986	143.2	17.4	100.0	40.4	14.1	81.2	183.6	16.5	95.9

Statistical Abstract(s) of Israel
* % NR is percent of non–residential of total building

Jewish settlements in the Territories. There are no official statistics for such building. There is, however, (see Table 4.3.2) a sub-heading for investment in building and construction works (over 60 per cent of total investment), but this includes housing, its major component. The non-residential building and construction as a proportion of total investment in building and construction is an estimated 28 per cent, while in Israel this exceeds 42 per cent.

In the absence of other information it may be concluded that non-residential construction lags far behind housing construction in the Territories or of non-residential construction in Israel. There is no public non-residential building in the West Bank and little in Gaza.

Of non-residential civil engineering works, construction of roads in the West Bank is the most important. Nevertheless, "road alignment and construction reflect the geopolitical planning strategies of the Israeli authorities in control more than the transportation needs of the West Bank population."[19] There were 1,682 km. of paved roads in the West Bank in 1985. Only 350 km. of these were constructed (paved) under Israeli rule. Nearly all of this addition (i.e. since 1967) has been in Class One roads which doubled in length to 731 km. These represent a decline in per capita road availability since 1967. Israeli partisan interests (e.g. security and Israeli settlements) account for much of road construction in the Territories. The 951 km. of Class Two roads which serve purely Arab needs were left virtually unchanged under Israeli occupation, despite the population increase. In effect, there has been a decline in paved roads relative to population. "Road density relative to 1,000 population was 1.8 in 1985 according to the WBDP population estimate, compared to 2.3 in 1967 (excluding urban areas)."[19] The new master plan for roads (1983-84) placed special emphasis on paving convenient roads for new settlements located near the metropolitan areas of Jerusalem and Tel Aviv to the city centers.

4.5 Cement and Other Building Materials

A large part of the construction industry is supplied by domestic products. This does not, however, include cement, the main building material.

Building-materials industries tend to cluster around areas of high population growth. They have enjoyed very rapid growth and remarkable technological advances. Employment grew almost tenfold between 1967 and 1986 to include almost 3,000 workers in the West Bank alone[20], excluding wood industries.

One of the most widely-produced local building materials is wood and wood products. Note, however, that the wood itself is imported. This sub-sector consists of some 500 enterprises in the West Bank and 350 in Gaza, mostly small, averaging 2.5 to 3 workers per unit. Their owners are mostly master carpenters assisted by relatives. The revenue generated per (officially) employed person is less than $5,000 per annum. Besides supplying wooden parts and carpentry services and craftsmen for the construction industry, they include many manufacturers of wooden furniture. They are not highly mechanized.

Quarrying is one important area in which most of the firms are operated with advanced machinery; hence manual labor and the need for additional workers are reduced. Much of their output is exported to Jordan and Israel. "Over half of the stone quarries are in the Hebron area, while over half of the stone-cutters are in the Ramallah and Bethlehem sub-districts" (see Table 4.5.1 for distribution of construction industries by sub-districts).[21]

There are some 500 small firms, mostly making cement products (420 firms), but also producing marble, bricks and tiles. They involve some 1,200 workers. These products are mainly for local consumption but some are also exported to Jordan and Israel. Three hundred of the 420 firms making cement products with some 900 workers are located in the Gaza Strip. Note the difference in the above-mentioned data[22] and in the two tables (4.5.1 and 4.5.2) which come from different sources. These are, however, marginal and the data serve only as indicators of the industry.

The cement for these industries is entirely imported from Israel. For over a decade, local Arab investors have attempted to establish a cement plant in Hebron with a capacity of some 600,000 tons per annum[23]. Note that local WB/GS demand for cement (1986 and 1987) is around 475,000 tons[24]. Permission to establish the plant has consistently been

Table 4.5.1

Construction Industries in the West Bank, 1987*

Sub-Distr.	Stone Quarries		Stone Cutters		Blocks & Tiles		Reading Mix Concrete		Gravel Quarries	
	Plants	Reg. Workers	Plants	Reg. Workers	Plants	Reg. Workers	Plants	Reg. Workers	Plants	Reg. Workers
Jenin	25	88	29	136	20	51	–	–	2	15
Nablus	27	95	36	219	34	198	2	38	3	20
Tulkarem	22	77	11	56	53	244	–	–	3	20
Ramallah	15	55	52	260	**	**	2	31	10	70
Bethlehem	10	35	79	347	12	98	3	61	1	7
Hebron	126	440	38	180	16	53	1	6	2	18
TOTAL	225	790	245	1198	135	644	8	136	21	180

* Source: Civil Administration; Published in "The West Bank and Gaza Atlas" WBDP, 1988.
** Not available

Table 4.5.2

West Bank and Gaza Building Materials and Wood Manufacturing

Area	Nablus		Ramallah El Birah		Hebron		Tulkarem & Qalqilya		Jenin		East Jerusalem & Bethlehem		Gaza Strip		Total	
Industry	Plants	Empl.	Plants	Empl.	Plants	Empl.	Plants	Empl.	Plants	Empl.	Plants	Empl.	Plants	Empl.	Plants	Empl.
Wood and Carpentry	142	274	37	76	50	165	34	301	27	33	170	193	90	838	519	1379
Cement Products	46	127	16	84	11	31	26	94	9	30	–	–	302	927	429	1053
Marble, Bricks & Tiles	8	36	8	20	8	31	4	15	12	26	32	45	–	–	69	173

Source: UNIDO, "Survey of the Manufacturing Industries in the West Bank and Gaza Strip" June, 1984; extracted from "Industrialization in the West Bank and Gaza," Simcha Bahiri, WBDP, 1987.

refused by both the Israeli and Jordanian authorities. The entire need for portland (grey) cement is purchased from Israel's sole cement company.

There was a steadily-declining percentage increase in each year in WB/GS cement consumption during the period 1968 to 1979, but this is partly normal as their starting base was low[25]. The average per annum increase in that period was over 15 per cent. Between 1979 and 1981 cement demand was stagnant. In 1982, as compared with 1981, there was an approximate drop of 20 per cent in building activity[26], a 17 per cent drop in cement consumption and a 27 per cent drop in building starts. This level of cement consumption – an indicator of building activity – continued in 1983 and 1984 with around 365,000 tons per annum. The level rose in 1985 to 395,000 tons (8 per cent) and again (20 per cent) in 1986 to 475,000 tons. This level continued in 1987. Note that nearly all of the cement used in the West Bank and Gaza, apart from industry, is from sacks. Bulk cement, which is hardly used, is an indicator of technological progress.

The average per capita consumption in the WB/GS is increasing (in contrast to that in Israel which has been decreasing since a high in 1972 of 580 kg. to a level of around 430 kg. per capita) and in 1987 of around 345 kg. per capita[27].

Most of the more sophisticated building materials and equipment are imported from or through Israel.

4.6 Housing Conditions

The standard of housing conditions in the West Bank and Gaza may be investigated by various indicators. Abu Kishk and Ghurani[28] suggest the following factors:

— type and quality of facilities in existing housing units;
— number of people per room;
— rental as a percentage of income; and
— the supply of new housing units.

As their data is based on statistics from 1976 and earlier, they find that facilities are mostly substandard and inadequate, an occupancy density of over three persons per room, an implication that most dwellers rent their houses for half their income, and a decline in available housing – this last being due to a reduction in building and to high rates of deterioration and abandonment of the older housing units. In this section we will update their findings and in the next section attempt to determine household dwelling requirements.

Despite the recent relative stagnation, the standard of living in the households in the West Bank and Gaza has continued to rise. This is measured (see Tables 4.6.1: WB, and 4.6.2: GS) by possession of certain household facilities and ownership of dwelling. The major characteristic of the two tables is that a comparison of 1985 with 1974 indicates that there was a significant improvement by 1985 in the possession of household facilities. The percentage improvements are even greater for villages in the West Bank and refugee camps in the Gaza Strip. Facility-possession in towns in both areas reached a very high proportion by 1985 – for some items nearly total possession. A study of the two tables will be self-explanatory. An examination of households possessing durable goods would show the same pattern of increase.

Ownership of dwellings in the villages in the West Bank reached 91 per cent as compared with only 67.8 per cent in the towns. This, however, is an improvement from 11 years earlier, with 48.5 per cent in the towns. In urban areas in the Gaza Strip this reaches 89.1 per cent – up from 71.6 per cent. No data is given for ownership of dwellings in Gaza because of difficulties in definition. One of the reasons for such relatively high ownership of dwellings in the Territories is that real estate is a traditional form of investment in the Arab world. The trend shows a steady growth in ownership. The proportion as shown in Tables 4.6.1 and 4.6.2 of rented dwellings of four per cent in Gaza (including refugee camps) and 11.5 per cent in the West Bank (down from 9.8 per cent and 16.7 per cent respectively in 1974) belie the implication of a high proportion of total income for rent.

Despite the high rate of ownership of facilities, durable goods and of dwellings, the average number of persons per household in the Territories has remained relatively constant since 1975 (6.55 in 1975 versus 6.51 in 1987). Nevertheless, there has been an increase in the number of rooms per household from 2.42 in 1975 to 2.98 in 1987 (see Table 4.6.3).

This results in an average of 2.19 persons per room in the Territories (2.13 in the WB and 2.27 in the GS as against 2.79 and 2.56 respectively in 1975). The reduction in the most overcrowded households, e.g. those with a population density of three or more per room, declined from over 50 per cent in 1975 to under 35 per cent in 1987 (as compared with an estimated 4 per cent or less in Israel)[29].

While the annual rate of growth of housing (1977 to 1987) by area increased for both the West Bank (4.1 per cent) and the Gaza Strip (1.5 per cent), the rate of growth for housing units increased only 2.5 per cent for the West Bank and actually declined (-1.0 percent) in Gaza (see Table 4.6.4). This difference represents the growth in size of housing units by an average of 1.9 per cent per annum. As the number of inhabitants remained the same, the area available per inhabitant increased representing an improvement in housing conditions. Nevertheless, serious overcrowding (e.g. over three persons per room) remains. The median housing density fell, however, between 1975 and 1987 from 3.0 to 2.5 persons per household[30].

The supply of housing units during a given period of time is equal to the number of units at the beginning of the period plus the number of units completed during that period less the number of units depleted during that period. Although there has not been a study of housing conditions in the past decade, it is estimated (based on statistics derived from data on average size of population and average number of persons per household) that the net supply of housing has increased from 166,800 in 1975 to 215,700 in 1987 (see Table 4.6.3). This represents a rate of increase for the (derived) number of households of 2.2 per cent per annum – a slight improvement over the official population increase.

The average number of rooms per dwelling (household) increased from 2.42 to 2.98, an increase of 23 per cent between 1975 and 1987. The increase in the West Bank was far higher (nearly 34 percent) (see Table 4.6.3). The actual number of rooms alone increased by nearly 59 per cent over the period, a rate of growth equal to 3.9 per cent per annum.

The number of persons per room declined in the West Bank from 2.79 in 1975 to 2.13 in 1987, an improvement of nearly 24 per cent. For the Gaza Strip, the decrease was only 11.3 per cent, from 2.56 to 2.27. The average for the two areas shows an improvement of 19 per cent, from 2.7 to 2.19 persons per room. Clearly, there has been significant reduction in overcrowding.

The average net size of a new dwelling in 1987 for the Territories was 133 sq.m. as compared with only 110 sq.m. in 1977, representing an annual growth rate in size of dwelling of 1.9 per cent (see Table 4.6.4). Nevertheless, there were

Table 4.6.1

Household Facilities and Ownership of Dwellings By Selected Type of Localities In the West Bank (Percentage of All Households)

	Villages			Towns			Total		
	1985	1981	1974	1985	1981	1974	1985	1981	1974
Household Facilities									
Kitchens	75.8	66.8	54.3	93.4	89.0	84.0	80.9	74.5	64.1
Electric or Gas Cooker	83.9	69.0	–	95.6	87.4	–	86.6	74.6	–
Heating Facility	98.2	97.9	98.5	97.2	97.4	98.6	97.3	97.3	98.5
Internal Running Water	49.5	29.3	9.8	91.0	79.0	60.9	61.6	44.9	23.5
Tap in Courtyard	15.3	20.4	13.3	7.3	13.4	17.6	13.6	20.4	17.0
Bathroom Only	36.5	27.6	16.5	50.1	53.6	45.8	39.3	34.8	23.7
Bathroom & Toilet	7.8	12.6		27.6	20.1		13.3	15.7	
Toilet	85.5	78.4	69.0	99.8	97.6	98.8	90.1	85.3	78.8
of which Flush	22.0	12.9	6.8	51.7	35.1	25.7	29.6	19.8	12.5
Water Heating for Bathing	99.7	99.6	–	99.9	99.2	–	99.8	99.5	–
of which Solar	39.2	24.0	–	60.7	41.8	–	44.2	29.4	–
of which Electric or Gas	1.5	3.5	–	1.4	6.6	–	1.5	4.6	–
Electricity Around Clock	46.4	28.9	27.6	98.2	95.8	91.5	63.1	50.6	45.8
Electricity Part of Day	41.0	46.5	–	1.0	1.5	–	28.1	31.0	–
Ownership of Dwelling									
Owned	91.0	91.5	85.9	67.8	58.2	48.5	–	–	–
Not owned but no rent paid	2.5	3.1	6.8	2.3	3.2	7.9	2.3	3.0	10.2
Rented	6.2	4.6	7.3	29.8	38.1	43.6	11.5	13.5	16.7

Statistical Abstract of Israel, 1987

significant differences between the two – e.g. the size of a West Bank unit was only 83 per cent of that in Gaza in 1977 and 88 per cent in 1987. While there was also an actual growth in Gaza of residential area built over the decade of 22 per cent, the number of dwellings completed declined by 10 per cent. In the West Bank both area and dwellings increased by 44 per cent and 19 per cent respectively.

New construction was viewed in per capita terms for the

Table 4.6.2

Household Facilities & Ownership of Dwellings By Selected Type of Localities in the Gaza Strip (Percentage of All Households)

	Refugee Camps			Towns			Total		
	1985	1981	1974	1985	1981	1974	1985	1981	1974
Household Facilities									
Kitchens	94.3	97.1	82.5	95.8	97.4	85.6	94.3	96.4	82.5
Electric or Gas Cooker	83.7	70.2	–	90.8	72.8	–	87.2	72.0	–
Heating Facility	42.9	53.3	77.4	57.6	68.0	78.1	51.7	64.1	78.6
Internal Running Water	68.5	39.7	3.4	83.2	63.1	25.7	75.1	51.4	13.9
Tap in Courtyard	29.4	56.9	57.8	15.0	33.7	62.3	22.1	44.0	61.5
Bathroom Only	58.3	33.6	11.5	61.6	53.1	26.5	58.3	44.4	18.3
Bathroom & Toilet	7.5	17.4		17.1	16.6		14.3	16.8	
Toilet	97.4	99.0	77.6	98.7	98.3	86.2	97.3	97.8	79.0
of which Flush	64.1	2.8	0.4	78.4	24.5	13.7	71.6	14.4	7.3
Water Heating for Bathing	99.9	99.9	–	99.7	99.5	–	99.8	99.8	–
of which Solar	65.0	35.3	–	75.9	52.0	–	70.3	44.4	–
of which Electric or Gas	0.3	0.4	–	1.0	0.1	–	0.7	0.3	–
Electricity Around Clock	94.4	83.9	14.1	93.7	89.2	56.8	92.8	88.5	34.5
Electricity Part of Day	0.7	0.0	–	0.1	0.0	–	0.7	0.0	–
Ownership of Dwelling									
Owned	–	–	–	89.1	80.8	71.6	–	–	–
Not owned but no rent paid	0.2	0.0	8.9	1.7	2.7	9.6	2.0	1.3	8.7
Rented	0.5	0.0	1.7	7.6	14.0	18.9	4.0	6.4	9.8

Source: Statistical Abstract of Israel, 1987

most recent four year average (1984-1987) and for incremental growth (see Table 4.6.5). Note that there are significant differences between the West Bank and Gaza Strip. Per capita total finishes in terms of area in the West Bank are twice as large as in Gaza and well over double that for non-residential building. Although for housing in terms of area, the ratio is slightly less than double, in terms of number of units the ratio approaches 2.4 times. The number of new rooms per dwelling is, however, greater in the Gaza Strip, 4.16 versus 3.73 (see Table 4.6.5). As the per capita building is less in Gaza, the ratio of population growth per new room

Table 4.6.3

Housing Conditions in the WB/GS in 1975 & 1987*

	West Bank	Gaza Strip	WB + GS
		1 9 7 5	
Average Population	672,450	419,750	1,092,200
Households	105,070	61,730	166,800
Rooms**	240,710	163,810	404,600
Persons per Household	6.40	6.80	6.55
Persons per Room	2.79	2.56	2.70
Rooms per Household	2.29	2.65	2.42
		1 9 8 7	
Average Population	848,850	554,550	1,403,400
Households	130,390	85,310	215,700
Rooms**	398,470	244,160	642,630
Persons per Household	6.51	6.50	6.51
Persons per Room	2.13	2.27	2.19
Rooms per Household	3.06	2.86	2.98
	% Difference 1987 over 1975		
Average Population	26.2	32.1	28.5
Households	24.1	38.2	29.3
Rooms**	65.5	49.0	58.8
Persons per Household	1.7	-4.4	-0.6
Person per Room	-23.7	-11.3	-19.3
Rooms per Household	33.6	7.9	23.1

* Source: Statistical Abstract of Israel, 1988, Jerusalem
** Rooms are derived from the above and five or more rooms per dwelling are calculated as six

Table 4.6.4
Comparative Analysis of Dwellings: Units,
Area and Size in 1977 & 1987*

	West Bank	Gaza Strip	WB + GS
		1 9 7 7	
Completed Area - M^2	504,800	181,400	686,200
Completed Dwellings: Units	4,497	1,387	5,884
Net Size - M^{2**}	104.4	126.0	110.0
		1 9 8 7	
Completed Area - M^2	769,100	221,500	990,600
Completed Dwellings: Units	5,740	1,247	6,987
Net Size - M^{2**}	127.1	144.5	133.0
	% Per Annum Growth Rate 1977-1987		
Completed Area - M^2	4.3	2.0	3.7
Completed Dwellings - M^2	2.5	-1.0	1.7
Net Size - M^{2**}	2.0	1.4	1.9

* Source: Statistical Abstract(s) of Israel, CBS, Jerusalem
** Net size is less than Area : Units (or gross size) and is taken
   directly from the Statistical Abstracts.

or new dwelling is greater there (3.06 per room versus 1.19 and 12.70 versus 4.43 respectively). This is caused by a higher population growth rate in Gaza (3.3 versus 2.7 per cent) and a lower rate of growth in new building, despite the greater number of rooms per dwelling in Gaza.

The average number of persons per room in the Territories in 1987 was 2.19 (see Table 4.6.3). The recent (1984-1987) growth in population and housing (see Table 4.6.5) resulted in an additional growth of 1.62 persons per new room – a reduction in the average number of persons per room.

There are no reliable up-to-date studies[31] for determining the present average size of a housing unit. For new houses this is 133 sq.m., and this has shown a steady growth. The accumulated stock of houses which were of smaller size may not exceed an average of 95 to 100 sq.m., say 98 sq.m. For a unit with 6.51 persons this equals around 15 sq.m. per person. Note that this is only an estimate based on a cursory analysis of incomplete data, mostly from CBS sources.

Table 4.6.5

New Construction per Capita in the WB/GS: Average 1984-1987*

	West Bank	Gaza Strip	WB + GS
Average			
Population Growth	22,050	17,400	39,450
Population	815,900	529,300	1,345,200
Total Building Finishes - M^2	820,900	265,700	1,086,600
Residential Building Finishes-M^2	676,400	227,720	904,120
Non-Housing Building Finishes-M^2	144,500	37,980	182,480
No. of New Dwellings	4,980	1,370	6,350
No. of New Rooms	18,591	5,694	24,285
Rooms in Dwelling	3.73	4.16	3.82
Rate			
Total Finishes per 1000 population - M^2	1,006	502	808
Residential Finishes per 1000 population - M^2	829	430	672
Non-Residential Finishes per 1000 population - M^2	177	72	136
Dwellings per 1000 population	6.11	2.59	4.72
Rooms per 1000 population	22.79	10.76	18.05
Population Growth per Room	1.19	3.06	1.62
Population Growth per Dwelling	4.43	12.70	6.21
Average Population Growth Rate %	2.70	3.30	2.90

* Source: Statistical Abstract(s) of Israel, CBS

4.7 Housing Needs

Housing needs represent the real demand for housing. While we will assume that social needs or demands in the Territories will exceed the irreducible biological demand, these basic needs in terms of area per person or family and number of people per room are to some degree arbitrary.

While the WBDP Atlas[32] estimates a population somewhat larger than the CBS (see Appendix 1), we will utilize the official CBS data in full awareness that population (but not necessarily population growth rate) may be over 20 per cent greater. For this section we assume that there are 1.4 million Arab residents of the Territories excluding East Jerusalem for the base year of 1987. We further consider the housing needs for 1997. That year will also be the year chosen for our alternative scenarios, later discussed.

There was an officially present population of approximately 1.4 million Arab residents in the Territories in 1987. As there was an average of 6.51 persons per household and, assuming each household represents one occupied dwelling, then there were 215,500 occupied dwellings, or 1,404,000 : 6.51. This makes no provision for unoccupied dwellings.

Assuming that the estimated average size of dwelling of 98 sq.m. was reasonable, then there are a net of 21 million sq.m. of housing (98 x 215,500.) This represents around 15 sq.m. per person. We will use this figure as the basis for social needs for housing, although Abu Kishk[33] feels that 12.5 sq.m. could be adequate. This, however, does not take into account the present higher rate per person being built nor for the undesirability of reducing average living standards. If, however, the housing figures are taken as actual and we use the WBDP Atlas population estimates, then the present average space per capita would be roughly 12.5 sq.m.

In order to generate the amount of housing needed (basic and social) and the amount of additional housing to reach these totals for 1987 and 1997, see Tables 4.7.1 and 4.7.2. The main assumptions (see footnotes in Tables) for an analysis of basic needs and social needs differ. Basic needs involve an average of 6.5 persons per housing unit, 12.5 sq.m. area per person, 2.71 rooms per house, 2.4 persons per room, 30 sq.m. per room, and 81.25 sq.m. per housing unit.

Social needs require an improvement as follows: 6.0 persons per room, 15.0 sq.m. per person, 3 rooms per housing unit, 2 persons per room, 30 sq.m. per room and 90.0 sq.m. average per housing unit.

In 1987, there were on average 5.86 persons per household in Israel's Arab sector. The 1970 level (6 persons per household) for this sector was chosen as the social minimum for size of household in the West Bank 10 years hence. By that time, Israel's Arab population will have further reduced the average size of household, possibly to 5.5 persons. There is no up-to-date data for number of person per room in Israel's Arab sector, but two was considered the maximum allowed to achieve minimum social conditions. Six persons per household with three rooms yields two persons per room.

The present 6.5 persons per household is probably the maximum that will be reached. The present 2.2 persons per room is midway between the estimated basic and social needs, i.e. 2.4 and 2.0 persons per room.

The present size of unit is an estimated 98 sq.m. as compared to 133 sq.m. for new housing. We will take Abu Kishk's 12.5 sq.m. per person for minimum basic needs; multiplied by 6.5 persons, equals 81.25 sq.m. This compares with 90 sq.m. for minimum social needs. The object of this exercise is to determine how many extra units and extra building area completions are needed at present for both conditions; and how many are required to be built over the next decade under varying hypotheses. The latter range from present (1987) CBS population estimates to WBDP

Table 4.7.1

Theoretical Housing Needs for Various Conditions: 1987 & 1997*

	Population (1,000)**	TOTAL Basic Needs***		Social Needs****	
		1,000 Units	1,000 M^2	1,000 Units	1,000 M^2
CBS Based 1987	1,400	215.3	17,500	233.3	21,000
CBS Based 1997 – No Return	1,800	276.9	22,500	300.0	27,000
CBS Based 1997 – Refugee Return	2,550	392.3	31,900	425.0	38,200
WBDP Based 1987	1,720	264.6	21,500	286.7	25,800
WBDP Based 1997 – No Return	2,200	338.5	27,500	366.7	33,000
WBDP Based 1997 – Refugee Return	3,130	481.6	39,100	521.6	46,900

 * Sources for basic data: Statistical Abstract(s) of Israel; WBDP Atlas; Abu Kishk and Ghurani; Sadler and Abu Kishk. Note that these are neither forecasts nor scenarios.
 ** Alternative existing and projected populations are based first on the differences between the CBS and WBDP estimates, then on the possibility of there being no massive return of refugees or a return of 600,000 over a decade.
 *** Basic needs involve 6.5 persons per housing unit, 12.5 square meters per person, 2.71 rooms per house, 2.4 persons per room, 30 square meters per room, and 81.25 square meters per housing unit.
 **** Social needs involve 6.0 persons per housing unit, 15.0 square meters per person, 3 rooms per house, 2 persons per room, 30 square meters per room, and 90.0 square meters per housing unit.

present population estimates. Two conditions for possible population 10 years hence are considered for each scenario: (a) that no refugees will return; and (b) that 600,000 refugees will return to a separate Palestinian entity (see Section 6.4). For the *status quo* scenario for both population possibilities, we assumed a 2.5 per cent population growth rate. For the refugee-return scenario, the calculated population growth rate was 6.2 per cent per annum.

The calculations in the tables (4.7.1 and 4.7.2) are neither forecasts nor scenarios. They are rather an attempt to determine the quantity of housing required to meet minimum basic and social needs at present and a decade hence, under various hypotheses of population and population growth. In contrast, alternative scenarios which involve

Table 4.7.2

Additional Housing Required to Meet Basic and Social Needs*

	Population (1,000)**	ADDITION Basic Needs***		REQUIRED Social Needs***	
		1,000 Units	1,000 M²	1,000 Units	1000 M²
CBS Based 1987	1,400	-0.2 (surplus)	-3,500 (surplus)	17.8	–
CBS Based 1997 – No Return	1,800	104.5	5,700	127.6	10,200
CBS Based 1997 – Refugee Return	2,550	219.9	15,100	252.6	21,400
WBDP Based 1987	1,720	49.1	8,900	71.2	4,800
WBDP Based 1997 – No Return	2,200	200.2	14,900	237.4	20,400
WBDP Based 1997 – Refugee Return	3,130	309.2	22,300	392.3	34,300

* Sources for basic data: Statistical Abstract(s) of Israel; WBDP Atlas; Abu Kishk and Ghurani; Sadler and Abu Kishk. Note that these are neither forecasts nor scenarios.
** See note 2 in Table 4.7.1
*** See notes 3 and 4 in Table 4.7.1. Note the existing situation or starting point of 215,500 housing and 21,000,000 net sq. m. of housing. Also note that we use a 2 per cent replacement and deterioration coefficient (of starting condition) for basic needs and a 4 per cent coefficient for social needs. Abu Kishk use a 7 per cent coefficient for need based on the low standard of existing housing but this is exaggerated. The 2 per cent basis works out at 4,300 houses per annum replaced, representing 420,000 sq. m. per annum. The 4 per cent represent 8,600 houses and 840,000 sq. m. respectively.

possible outcomes given various political developments (on CBS population statistics) are dealt with in Section 6.

For 1987, on CBS population estimates for basic needs there is an insignificant surplus (200 units) in number of dwellings and a significant surplus in area required (3.5 million sq.m.). For social needs while there is a present shortage of 17,800 houses, there is no shortage in square meters required, demonstrating that existing size of houses are higher than minimum social needs.

The additional rate of growth required to meet basic and social needs is shown in Table 4.7.3. For the ordinary (CBS) growth scenario the growth rate for number of units required by 1997 is 2.5 per cent for basic needs and 3.4 per cent for social needs. For a refugee-return scenario, this is 6.2 per cent and 7 per cent respectively. For the WBDP population hypothesis, while the rate of growths required is higher, it is in the realm of practical possibility.

At present, a housing crisis of considerable magnitude exists in the West Bank and Gaza. It does not appear likely that the family units concerned are capable now, nor in the foreseeable future, of solving the housing problem. Even if there is a separate entity with its own administration, the problem will remain, as there will be a large number of

Table 4.7.3

Percentage Rate of Growth Required to Meet Needs in 1997*

	Population (1000)**	Basic Needs** %		Social Needs** %	
		Units	Area	Units	Area
CBS Based 1997 – No Return	1,800	2.5	0.7	3.4	2.5
CBS Based 1997 – Refugee Return	2,550	6.2	4.3	7.0	6.2
WBDP Based 1997 – No Return	2,200	4.6	2.7	5.5	4.6
WBDP Based 1997 – Refugee Return	3,130	8.4	6.4	9.2	8.4

* Sources: Same as Tables 4.7.1 and 4.7.2
** Footnotes same as Tables 4.7.1 and 4.7.2

returnees requiring housing. To provide housing not only for those who now require it, to eliminate refugee camps, to cater for increases in population (natural or through immigration), to replace the increased number of housing units which will deteriorate, to raise the standard of housing and reduce overcrowding, would require not only a massive building effort over a period of a decade, but probably over a much longer period.

4.8 Building Patterns, Location and Density

As discussed in Chapter 5, it appears that apart from sectarian Israeli planning there is no comprehensive planning process in operation in the occupied Territories. This has the effect of generating unplanned built-up areas and urban sprawls. Nevertheless, around one-sixth of the total of the West Bank is planned built-up areas of which over two-fifths is Jewish-planned built-up area[34]. In the Gaza Strip, planned Jewish area is more limited. The most effective way that the Palestinians attempt to resist Israeli land seizures is through building activity on their lands[35].

Two common aspects of Arab building patterns are: (a) "ribbon development" – which are long and narrow built-up areas on both sides of access roads, and (b) single-family houses interspersed with large tracts of orchards and farmsteads[36].

The development along existing roads (ribbon development) is generally of lower population density than found in urban settlement[37]. The lowering of population density is also pronounced in villages transforming rural settlement structure from a compact high density model to a scattered one. Although purely compact rural areas are being transformed into integrated agricultural and urban/suburban residential entities, the entire area (southern West Bank) is becoming more difficult for introducing planned improvements in infrastructure (streets, sidewalks, sewers) and public transportation. Patterns of social behavior (village-dwellers' reluctance to leave their place of residence, tendency of young couples to build their residences on family-owned land and building to prevent Jewish land seizures) reinforce the trend to sub-urbanization[38].

Excluding purely agricultural land, the above form of

Table 4.8.1

Urban and Rural Population and Construction in the WB/GS in 1987*

	WEST BANK				GAZA STRIP				WB + GS			
	Pop.	Compl. Bldng. Area - M^2	Area per 1000 pop. M^2	% non-resident completions	Pop.	Compl. Bldng. Area - M^2	Area per 1000 pop. M^2	% non-resident completions	Pop.	Compl. Bldng. Area - M^2	Area per 1000 pop. M^2	% non-resident completions
Town/Urban	631,120	548,850	870	24.3	447,950	194,600	434	13.1	1,079,060	743,400	689	21.3
Village/Rural	436,750	382,000	875	7.4	185,610	55,900	301	6.3	623,370	437,900	702	7.3
Total	1,067,870	930,800	872	17.4	633,560	250,500	395	11.6	1,702,430	1,181,300	694	16.2
% Urban**	59.1	59.0	–	82.3	70.7	77.7	–	87.9	63.4	62.9	–	83.2
% Rural	40.9	41.0	–	17.7	29.3	22.3	–	12.1	36.6	37.1	–	16.8

* Sources: For Population the WBDP "Atlas" and for Building the Statistical Abstract of Israel
** % urban and rural for area per 1,000 population refer to percentages of absolute numbers

building results in a building density of 0.8 families per dunam, which at 6.5 persons per household, is 5.2 persons per dunam[39]. This compares with an average of 3.0 persons per dunam for Arab settlement in the southern half of the West Bank excluding East Jerusalem[40]. The population density per dunam ranged from a low of 1.2 persons in the Jordan sub-district including Jericho (with its relatively empty refugee camps) to 4.0 for the Bethlehem sub-districts. The Ramallah and Bethlehem sub-districts had a density of 2.6 and 3.2 respectively. The 3.0 persons per

Table 4.8.2

West Bank Geographical Areas, Population & Densities in 1987*

	Population	Area Sq.Km.	Persons per Sq. Km.	% Increase 1967 – 1987
Rural				
Yaabad	56,768	261	217.5	73.7
Tubas	77,526	399	194.3	79.3
Anabta	53,720	272	197.5	63.0
Azzun	30,712	239	128.5	77.4
Sumaria	103,088	599	172.1	67.4
Um Saffa	80,975	498	162.6	71.8
Jiftlik	2,665	567	4.7	46.8
Auja	3,577	490	7.3	138.4
Jerusalem Out.	86,830	506	171.6	83.1
Tarqumiya	75,306	404	186.4	90.7
Yatta	59,950	550	109.0	97.2
Desert	0	506	0.0	–
Total Rural	631,117	5,291	119.3	76.8
Urban				
Jenin	26,677	8	3,334.6	94.1
Tulkarem	37,236	14	2,659.7	94.5
Qalqilya	18,972	8	2,371.5	112.5
Nablus Con.	114,102	31	3,680.7	76.7
Jericho	15,269	11	1,388.1	120.3
Jerusalem Con.	135,605	108	1,255.6	97.8
Hebron Con.	88,893	44	2,020.3	100.4
Total Urban	436,754	224	1,949.8	93.1
Grand Total	1,067,871	5,515	193.6	83.1

* Source: The West Bank and Gaza Atlas

dunam in 1984 compares with 4.7 in 1967. In terms of housing units per dunam, there was an improvement of 46 per cent, from 1.0 unit per dunam in 1967 to 0.54 in 1984, as more area was allocated to building.[41]

Construction in Bethlehem and Ramallah was strengthened by the administrative separation of East Jerusalem from the functional urban region areas in the southern West

Table 4.8.3
Gaza Strip Arab Localities, Status, Population
Area and Density in 1986*

	Status**	Population	Built-Up Area (Dunams)	Density = Population Per Built-up Dunam
Urban				
(inc. Urban Refugee Camps)				
Gaza and Shati	MC, RC	235,277	12,000	19.6
Deir al Balah	MC	32,420	5,555	5.8
Khan Yunis	MC	98,374	11,840	8.3
Rafah	MC,RC	81,876	7,985	10.3
Total		447,445	37,380	12.0
"Rural" Refugee Camps				
(inc. combined VC + RC)				
Beit Lehia + Jabalia	VC,RC	76,430	6,600	12.3
Bureij	RC	16,890	910	18.6
Muazi	RC	12,083	745	16.2
Nusseirat	RC	30,093	1,070	28.1
Total		140,496	9,325	13.5
Rural (Village Councils)				
Beit Hannun	VC	12,455	3,680	3.4
Zawaida	VC	2,168	930	2.3
Karara	VC	2,183	(scattered)	–
Bani Suhaila	VC	13,642	2,300	5.9
Khazaa	VC	4,091	1,000	4.0
Abassan Kabira	VC	8,795	2,580	3.4
Abassan Saghira	VC	1,835	730	2.5
Total		46,119	11,220	4.1
Grand Total		634,060	57,925	10.7

* West Bank and Gaza Atlas
** MC = Municipal Council; RC = Refugee Camp; VC = Village Council

Bank, which generated a movement of residents and businesses across the city line into those contiguous areas. Furthermore, several Jewish settlements in the region stimulated Arab construction around their peripheries[42]. These movements are reflected in revised population statistics[43].

Built-up areas in the southern West Bank (representing a total area of 3,600 sq. km. out of 5,500 sq. km. – 65 per cent) accounted for 136,900 dunam (137 sq. km.) in 1984, as compared with only 62,600 dunam in 1967, a growth of 119 per cent. This ranged from an increase of 180 per cent for Ramallah to only 13 per cent for the Jordan sub-district[44]. The increase is attributed to population growth, improved standard of housing, exchanging old houses for newer ones, savings and "steadfastness" or holding on to Arab land[45].

Kimhi et al.[46] state that according to aerial photographs for the southern West Bank, growth of built-up areas in the cities was relatively small as compared with the rural hinterlands. This even includes multi-storied buildings in villages.

Based on population estimates of the "Atlas"[47] and building statistics from the CBS annual, a comparison of urban and rural construction in 1987 was made (see Table 4.8.1) for both the West Bank and Gaza Strip. In the West Bank both population and building area were roughly 59 per cent urban and 41 per cent rural, so there was no significant difference in area completed per thousand persons – 872 sq.m. The one major difference was that nearly one-quarter of the urban buildings were non-residential as against only 7 per cent for rural areas.

In the Gaza Strip (where non-urban refugee camps are treated as being in rural areas), the population was 71 per cent urban and 29 per cent rural as against 78 per cent of completed building area being urban. The area built per thousand population was 434 sq.m. for the towns and 301 sq.m. for rural areas (870 and 875 respectively for the West Bank). Of this, 13 per cent was non-residential in towns and 6 per cent in rural areas. Here, there are significant differences between town and village and with the West Bank.

The breakdown by settlements and rural vs. urban population and densities is shown in Table 4.8.2. Rural areas comprise nearly 96 per cent of total area, yet they embrace only 59 per cent of the population and have a density of 119 persons per sq.km. (0.119 person per dunam). Urban areas represent 4 per cent of total area with 41 per cent of the population. They have a density of 1,950 persons per sq. km. (1.95 persons per dunam), or 16 times as much. Rural areas population over the 20-year period (1967 to 1987) grew nearly 77 per cent while urban area grew at a faster 93 per cent. Of the total combined area, 52 per cent are under Israeli control – both state and private.

In the Gaza Strip, of a total area of 365,000 dunam (365 sq. km.), there are 178,500 dunams in private Arab hands (48.9 per cent) and 36,000 dunams are state lands leased to Arabs (9.9 per cent). Thus, only around 60 per cent are under Arab control (215,000 dunam)[48]. Of this some 58,000 dunam or 27 per cent is built-up area (see Table 4.8.3). Urban built-up area represents less than 65 per cent, with the rest rural and non-municipal refugee camps. The four purely urban (municipal status) settlements contain over 70 per cent of the population with a population density of 12 persons per built-up dunam, as compared with 4.1 for rural village councils and 13.5 for "rural" refugee camps. The average for the Gaza Strip is 10.7 persons as against less than one quarter that for the West Bank. In terms of person per gross sq.km., these are 194 in the West Bank and 1,737 in the Gaza Strip (nine times as great).

5. Barriers To Construction Development

Despite an initial first decade (1967-77) of rapid progress, especially in construction, the West Bank and Gaza have in the '80s tended to lag behind in terms of their needs. For the past 21 years the development of the two Territories has largely been determined by the facts of occupation, the nature of their links with Israel and the Israeli military administration, the response of Jordan to the occupation and a number of indigenous factors[1]. Collectively these barriers – economic, administrative, political and cultural – have resulted in the continuation of the backward underdeveloped nature of construction and the paucity of non-residential building and public works[2]. It has been suggested[3] that Israeli "policy has been to keep the West Bank and Gaza Strip as markets for Israel's products, and as a supplier of cheap labor for Israel." While in reality this may be so, it has never been declared to be official Israeli policy. In practice, economic realities of unemployment and comparative wage-levels in the Territories have forced workers to seek employment in Israel – some 95,000 in 1986 or three-eighths of the labor force. Among construction workers, those employed in Israel exceed 45,000 which is over 70 per cent.

As in industry[4], there are many restrictions (both active and passive) on housing construction. On the passive side, there has been no systematic planning and zoning to accommodate the normal expansion of the Palestinian communities[5]. Also, there has been no construction of residential buildings for the Arab population by the public sector in the West Bank since 1968 and in the Gaza Strip since 1978, except for some housing projects for the resettlement of refugees in the Gaza Strip[6]. On the more active side, there are various legal and administrative restrictive barriers which will be discussed.

Planning for construction "in the West Bank is based on procedures set out in the Jordanian Town and Village Planning Law of 1966, as amended and in fact made meaningless by various military orders."[7] While in the very early years of Israeli occupation "procedures for physical planning and building permits were completely uncontrolled and unregulated,"[8] when the government realized the importance of the planning process for its rule over the West Bank it began to control the process. In 1970, it issued Order 393 "authorizing the military commander to forbid, hold, or set conditions for construction" and in 1971 Order 418 the "hierarchical" system of local, district, and national planning committees (customary in Israel and Jordan) was eliminated, and their customary composition was altered[9].

Meron Benvenisti, in describing this process of increasing Israeli control, writes:

powers were transferred to a Higher Planning Committee made up entirely of Israeli government representatives. District committees were eliminated and the licensing powers of the village councils transferred to the military government. The powers of the local planning committees, with responsibility within municipal boundaries, were drastically reduced. The High Planning Committee was authorized to amend, revoke or place conditions on any licence issued by a municipality, to issue licences itself, or grant exemptions and even to assume the powers of local committees. The involvement of local residents in the planning process became minimal and theoretical. The authorities' involvement was also limited at first and for all intents and purposes its efforts were confined to preventing construction in sensitive military areas."[10]

With the advent of the Likud to power in 1977, further restrictions were placed on the physical planning process for the Palestinians. This process reflects Israeli interests exclusively. The interests and needs of the Arab inhabitants are viewed as constraints to be overcome[11].

In recent years, despite overwhelming Israeli control, comprehensive regional plans for the West Bank prepared between 1982 and 1984 were not "deposited" legally. Nevertheless, the planning authorities act in accordance with them, often to the detriment of the indigenous population, as though they had been formally approved[12].

The devolution of the planning process for Jewish settlements gave them increased authority to control "State lands," "closed" areas and "requisitioned" areas. Planning bodies, by designating land uses, such as roads and other grids, as "public purposes" have the authority to decide upon their expropriation. In effect, this imposes a freeze in Palestinian land use in the vicinity of Jewish housing estates and makes possible the expropriation of all Palestinian lands needed to connect and serve the pockets of Jewish settlements. Jewish regional councils, representing less than 5 per cent of the population and area, have the monopoly for planning entire regions. Arab-owned land which is designated for Jewish public and developmental purposes (e.g. roads, watergrids, sewerage, garbage disposal, electricity, communication, industry, agriculture, and tourism), can be "expropriated for public purposes."[13]

In 1985, the physical planning unit which had been serving the Higher Planning Committee which had been part of the Ministry of Interior through a staff officer, was transferred to the Civil Administration's[14] "infrastructure branch." As this branch is responsible for the seizure and expropriation of land, the objective of the change becomes obvious[15].

"Once sufficient land for unlimited Jewish settlement was assured, statutory planning could be used to control the remaining areas, planning procedures being less controversial, but equally effective."[16]

The UNCTAD report states that "the restrictive practices of the occupying authorities, in terms of administrative obstacles to issuing building permits and the transfer of funds from abroad until 1985 (and again more recently with the intifada) have stifled local efforts and effectively barred a potentially large number of families from procuring decent housing."[17]

The vast majority of "administrative orders" of the authorities concern economic matters[18]. Applications that deal with housing in disputed zones might take several years to be processed and almost any changes require approval[19].

In 1970, Order 393 was issued concerning building in the West Bank. Under this order, any military commander "may prohibit construction or order a halt in construction if he believes it necessary for the security of the Israeli army in the area or to ensure public order." Such orders prohibiting building have been issued for areas around IDF camps and installations, around Jewish settlements, along a 200-meter strip along both sides of a main road, and even around whole settlement areas. In practice, orders have even been issued on built-up areas of Arab municipalities when authorities wish to curb building expansion[20].

Other regulations concerning land classifications which affect building in the West Bank and Gaza, are orders dealing with declaration of combat zones or fire zones as one would remain in a fire zone and consequently, no one would build in such an area. An order concerning the "Protection of Nature" (363, 1969) imposes severe restrictions on construction and land use in such areas[21].

Declaration of certain areas as State lands, closed areas or land requisition for military purposes further reduces the opportunity to build.

Besides lack of regional planning and restrictive laws on building, the state of infrastructure (transportation, water, telecommunication and electricity grids) for the Palestinian population in the Territories does little to promote rapid growth of needed residential building. (Roads have been discussed under non-residential building.) "Physical infrastructure is primarily planned to accommodate Israeli interests – especially settlement construction, Jewish agricultural construction and military needs. Water consumption per capita in Arab areas is estimated at half the Jewish consumption and electricity consumption per Arab family is less than half that calculated for a Jewish family."[22] Telephone exchanges have been closed down and their lines transferred to Israeli exchanges on both sides of the "Green Line." Only a small percentage of the Arab population's need for phones is met. The functioning of the Arab-owned Jerusalem Electric Company has been interfered with and supplies are erratic. "The Arab bus grid has remained unchanged during 21 years of Israeli administration...The inefficient system demonstrates the lack of regional planning, and neglect by central authority."[23] Central sewerage systems are insufficient to meet the needs for the local population[24].

Israeli fiscal policies and restrictions on Arab banks also play havoc with less qualified local entrepreneurs. These include devaluations and heavy tax payments (value-added tax, production tax, income tax, customs and other levies). This is further aggravated by poor bookkeeping practices of most building contractors which are often used as an excuse by tax authorities to impose excessively high tax levels. The lack of adequate credit facilities acts as a barrier to much potential housing construction.

Often, specific projects like the Hebron cement plant are administratively barred. Furthermore, the lack of adequate public budgets prevent most of the required public construction from taking place.

Only a fraction of the list of reasons for industrial non-expansion[25] affect the contracting sector, and they have some factors peculiar to their sector. Some of these factors have a political dimension. Capital shortages are influenced by whether approval is given to open banking facilities and allowing free flow of funds from abroad. Taxation has an even more direct political component than does granting or non-granting of permission to build.

In the relative absence of unemployment (prior to the intifada), obtaining qualified construction workers for WB/GS projects may sometimes be difficult, especially as these are more highly paid in Israel. Also there may on occasion be shortages of required building materials whether from Israel (cement)[26] or from domestic sources.

The area commander and through him the military, the Civil Administration, and eventually the Israel government, have assumed effective control over all aspects of life in which the law is involved, including commerce and construction. This includes being the registrar of lands and companies and having the powers of the Ministry of Construction and Housing[27].

In addition to powers transferred to the area commander or his nominees, others have been transferred to an "objection committee" drawn from a panel of reserve army officers with power in the field of land appropriation, income tax and objections on decisions of the registrar of companies. This committee impinges on commercial life and construction activities in a restrictive fashion, and there is little access to legal redress[28]. These bodies function to enhance Israel's security in the economic no less than the military field.

66

Building licences are closely regulated. This often involves exorbitant fees and lengthy processes, and their application in a restrictive manner[29].

The combined weight of not having their own economic administration, restrictive practices by Israel and a military administration, and more recently the intifada, all act together to limit greatly the potential for development of construction activities in the territories.

6. Ten-Year Alternative Construction Scenarios

6.1 General

The base year for the alternative projections presented is 1987. This is the latest year for which any data is available, part of it extrapolations from 1986. This is for the most part pre-intifada[1] or civil disturbances which began early in December 1987 (see Appendix 3). These troubles continued through all of 1988 and resulted in an estimated reduction of economic activity of at least 20 per cent over 1987 levels. Thus, all forecasts to 1997 have to assume, at least for 1988, such a reduction. While, for one of following projections (status quo), a partial continuation of these troubles after 1988 is assumed, the other two projections are based on rapidly overcoming the effects of the intifada after 1988. Note that these projections are not identical with the projections of housing needs from Section 4.6 but deal rather with likely events under different scenarios.

The three major potential scenarios for the Territories that have an impact on development and construction are:

— development under existing barriers or *status quo* (a conservative option) with a continuation of an intermittent intifada, albeit on a reduced basis;

— development under modified *status quo* with some barriers removed (a liberal or reformist option); and

— unrestricted development as in a separate WB/GS entity (a radical option).

These three scenarios or options are based on three broadly defined major alternative economic directions that the occupied Territories may possibly take. The first two are based on the scenario that for the coming decade the West Bank and Gaza will continue to be under Israeli occupation. The difference between the first (conservative) option and the second (reformist) option is that while the first implies a continuation of both the intifada and certain earlier trends *(status quo)*, the second involves a more "sympathetic or liberal occupation" with a reduction in the various restrictions by Israel, an early end to the intifada, and some degree of reform and local autonomy. The third (radical) option involves a major break or discontinuity with past trends, an immediate end to the intifada, and the establishment of a separate Palestinian entity in the West Bank and Gaza Strip – either as an independent state[2] or as a unit confederated with Jordan. This new entity might absorb some 400,000 to 800,000 refugees over the decade[3].

Taking the various scenarios in turn we will generate

Table 6.1.1

Ten-Year Alternative Economic Projections for the WB/GS

	1987 Estimated/ Actual	1997 Conservative	1997 Reformist	1997 Radical
Average Population & Employment (Thousands)				
Arab Population	1,400	1,790	1,825	2,550
Total Employment of WB/GS Residents	270	300	350	490
Employment in WB/GS	170	180	210	420
Distribution of GNP (1987 million US$)				
Gross National Product (GNP)	2,100	2,475	3,170	4,810
Government Consumption (G)	160	195	230	480
Private Consumption (P)	1,750	2,115	2,610	3,850
Investment (I)	540	650	940	1,860
Resources (R=G+P+I)	2,450	2,960	3,780	6,190
Import Surplus (IS=R-GDP)	850	1,070	1,170	1,380
Net Transfers (NT)	500	540	560	400
Gross Domestic Product (GDP=GNP-NT)	1,600	1,935	2,610	4,410
Per Capita Indices (1987 US$)				
GNP/Capita	1,500	1,380	1,735	1,885
GDP/Employment in WB/GS	9,410	10,750	12,430	10,500
Private Consumption Per Capita	1,250	1,200	1,430	1,510
Maximum 10 Year Growth-Rate (% per annum)				
Arab Population	2.5	2.5	2.7	6.3
Employment in WB/GS	2.5	1.7	2.6	9.2
GNP	3.5	1.7	4.2	8.6
Government Consumption	1.8	2.0	3.7	10.6
Private Consumption	3.5	1.9	4.1	8.2
Investment	1.5	1.9	5.7	13.2
GDP	3.8	1.9	5.0	10.7
GDP in Construction	4.0	2.8	6.0	13.1
Number of Housing Units Built	2.5	1.8	4.4	14.0

economic projections using the most logically consistent hypothesis. It should be emphasized that while there are not equal probabilities for each option, the conservative[4] and radical options do represent the two extreme but possible positions, while the reformist option represents an intermediate scenario. Furthermore, we will ignore Jewish settlement and building activity in the Territories[5] as these are outside the scope of this study.

In 1987 government consumption was less than 8 per cent of the GNP, private consumption over 83 per cent and investment, namely housing, over 26 per cent, leaving an import surplus of 40 per cent of the GNP. The 1987 data in Table 6.1.1 shows the 10-year annual growth rate for the previous decade for some critical indices. These range from 1.8 per cent to 4 per cent per annum. While for the next 10 years, these rates were higher than those of the intifada-

Table 6.1.2

Ten-Year Alternative GDP, Employment & Productivity For the WB/GS

	1987		1997 Conservative		1997 Reformist		1997 Radical	
	$ mill.	%	$ mill.	%	$ mill.	%	$ mill.	%
Gross Domestic Product	1,600	100.0	1,935	100.0	2,610	100.0	4,410	100.0
Agriculture	464	29.0	507	26.2	626	24.0	910	20.5
Industry	144	9.0	172	8.9	248	9.5	500	11.5
Construction	256	16.0	338	17.5	457	17.5	875	20.0
Services	736	46.0	918	47.4	1,279	49.0	2,125	48.0
	Thous.	%	Thous.	%	Thous.	%	Thous.	%
Employed	170	100.0	180	100.0	210	100.0	420	100.0
Agriculture	43	25.0	40	22.2	42	20.0	75	18.0
Industry	27	16.0	28	15.6	35	17.0	75	18.0
Construction	20	12.0	22	12.2	28	13.0	65	15.0
Services	80	47.0	90	50.0	105	50.0	205	49.0
	$	%	$	%	$	%	$	%
GDP/Employed	9,410	100.0	10,750	100.0	12,430	100.0	10,500	100.0
Agriculture	10,810	115.0	12,680	121.0	14,900	120.0	12,130	116.0
Industry	5,330	57.0	6,140	57.0	7,090	57.0	6,670	64.0
Construction	12,800	136.0	15,360	143.0	16,320	131.0	13,460	128.0
Services	9,200	98.0	10,200	95.0	12,180	98.0	10,370	99.0

based conservative option, the reverse is true for the other two options, especially the radical one.

Tables 6.1.1, 6.1.2, 6.1.3, and 6.1.4 show various aspects of possible developments for the three scenarios to 1997. They are not further discussed here, but are discussed in the section on each scenario, i.e. 6.2, 6.3 and 6.4.

Table 6.1.3

Forecast Household/Dwellings by Size and Density: Accumulated Totals, 1997

	1987 Conservative	1 9 9 7 Reformist	Radical
1. Population (average-thousands)	1,400	1,790	1,825	2,550
2. Households/Dwellings (thousands)	216	270	290	390
3. Rooms (thousands)	643	800	900	1,130
4. Persons per household	6.51	6.63	6.29	6.54
5. Rooms per household	2.98	2.96	3.10	2.90
6. Persons per room	2.19	2.24	2.03	2.26

Table 6.1.4

Forecast Household/Dwellings by Size, Density: and Productivity during 1997

	1987 Conservative	1 9 9 7 Reformist	Radical
1. Population (average-thousands)	1,400	1,790	1,820	2,550
2. No. of units completed	7,000	9,000	11,500	28,000
3. Area of housing completed (thousands M2)	990	1,170	1,540	3,640
4. No. of rooms completed	25,600	33,300	44,850	98,000
5. Average no. of rooms per new dwelling	3.65	3.7	3.9	3.5
6. Average size of dwelling (M2)	133.5	130.0	133.9	130.0
7. Total construction area (incl. non-housing) (thousands M2)	1,200	1,400	1,830	4,300
8. No. of construction workers (thousands)	20	22	28	65
9. M^2 per worker (productivity)	60.0	63.6	65.4	66.0

6.2 Development and Construction under Existing Constraints

Although the Territories have been occupied by Israel for over 21 years, the conservative scenario for the coming decade will depend heavily on extrapolating the events of the past pre-intifada decade (1977-1987) and modifying these to account for the effect of the disturbances, both of the events of 1988 and a continuing but reduced intifada over the rest of the decade. Note that our 1987 estimates and our 1997 possible forecast do not include East Jerusalem as separate data was not available. If it was included, we would have had to increase all parameters by around 10 per cent.

Note also that the 1987 data is common to all three projections. The population of 1.4 million Palestinian Arabs includes some 270,000 employed of which 170,000 were working in the West Bank and Gaza Strip.

The gross national product (GNP) in 1987 U.S. dollars (based on an over-valued shekel)[6] reached $2.1b. of which $1.6b. is the gross domestic product (GDP) which excludes the net transfer (mainly labor earnings) from Israel.

Using roughly similar but mainly lower growth indices for the next decade, as for the past decade, we generate the 1997 conservative scenario. Total population will increase nearly 28 per cent (2.5 percent per annum) to 1.79 million inhabitants, with a work force totaling 300,000 of which 180,000 will work in the Territories. The GNP and its components will increase at around 1.8 per cent per annum, to reach $2,475 million (i.e.$2.475 billion). This assumes no major difference from 1987 in the distribution of the GNP, and takes into account the intifada. This is the maximum growth rate possible for this scenario as a more serious intifada or war could lower these indicators.

While by 1997 the GNP will have grown to $2,475 million, the GDP will only reach $1,435 million. This represents an 18 per cent and a 21 per cent increase respectively, over the decade. The increase for the components of the GNP would also be similar. The per annum economic growth indices for this scenario range from 1.7 to 2.8 per cent for the period.

The distribution of the GNP would be 8 per cent for government consumption, 85 per cent for private consumption and 26 per cent, mostly housing, for investment, leaving an import surplus of 43 per cent.

The continuation of the slow rate of development is based on the assumption that given a stalemate in the political area, construction and housing will roughly follow the previous overall growth pattern at best[7].

Despite the continued but modest growth, construction activity as measured by cement consumption per capita would remain considerably lower than that in Israel, especially given the continuation of the intifada. Thus even allowing for considerable unofficial building[8], the structure of Arab housing and construction activity at the end of another decade of occupation will not be significantly altered. Construction will still comprise around 17 per cent of the GDP and 12 per cent of employment. The growth in construction would be some 2.8 per cent per annum. This is little more than the population growth rate. The characteristic backwardness of this sector will not be significantly altered. Note, however, that relative productivity (e.g. compared with other economic sectors) will remain over one-third higher than average. The low cost and availability of labor will work against modernizing this sector, thus exaggerating labor requirements[9].

The number of housing units that would be built in 1997 (7,500 units in 1987) would reach 9,000 units and the number of units constructed during the decade would be some 85,000. The total number of units in existence in 1997 (allowing for 20,000 deteriorated units taken out of use) would be some 270,000 units with a population density per unit of 6.63 (6.33 in 1987). This represents a reduction from the previous 2.5 per cent growth rate to only 1.8 per cent over the decade.

Nevertheless, in this, the conservative scenario, despite low investment in the productive sectors of the economy, the major investment area would be housing. Furthermore, in this situation the West Bank/Gaza area would continue to be integrated with the Israeli economy and remain dependent on it for most non-labor construction inputs[10]; and the per capita income gap with Israel would continue to remain wide − at four to one.

Building area per worker in construction, based on finishes, would be some 64 sq.m. (see Table 6.1.4).

Table 6.1.3 shows the projected accumulated statistics for housing in 1997. The column for the conservative scenario shows a growth in households of nearly 2.3 per cent per annum from 1987 to 270,000. Rooms would grow at a rate exceeding 2.2 per cent per annum to 800,000. There would be a slight worsening in persons per household in this scenario, rooms per household remain the same and population (persons) per room would also remain the same.

Table 6.1.4 shows the potential results for different scenarios in 1997. For the conservative scenario the number of housing units completed would rise by 2.5 per cent per annum over the decade while the area of housing would rise by only 1.5 per cent per annum. There would be no increase in the average number of rooms per new dwelling nor in the average size of dwelling. This scenario basically represents a continuation of the trends of the previous (1977-1987) decade and includes an estimated 5-10 per cent decline in construction output in 1988 over 1987. The rate of forecast increase for all parameters between 1988 and 1997 is naturally higher than those outlined above.

Note that all the above statistics as well as those in the rest of this chapter are based on CBS population statistics. If WBDP data (see Section 4.7) had been used, the forecast growth rates would have been higher.

6.3 Development and Construction under Reforms and/or Limited Autonomy

This reformist scenario is basically also a continuation of some degree of occupation by Israel, albeit with significant reforms in the political structure, such as Palestinian autonomy, a significant liberalization of economic development policies, and a lessening of restrictive economic barriers on the part of Israel. This also assumes that the Arab population of the Territories would cease their intifada and also accept the modest political and economic changes necessary for even this moderate political model to succeed. It represents the maximum growth that could result under some form of modified occupation and could be a step towards either a separate or "bi-national" entity. While important changes are involved, because of the continued occupation they would have a limited impact on economic development and construction activity. Nevertheless, they could have definite positive results within prescribed limits.

The population (see Table 6.1.1) would grow at a slightly faster rate of growth (2.7 per cent as versus 2.5 per cent), reaching 1,825,000 Arab inhabitants as fewer residents would leave for employment abroad and more return from abroad. The extra 35,000 inhabitants after a decade are, however, marginal. There would be an extra 30,000 workers of whom 6,000 workers (see Table 6.1.2) would be employed in construction in the Territories. These extra workers represent some 15 per cent of the manpower in the Territories and 25 per cent of these in construction.

The maximum GNP rate of growth would be considerably higher at 4.2 per cent as compared with 1.7 per cent under the status quo, and would reach $3,170 million (versus $2,475 million)[11]. In per capita terms, this would reach $1,735 which would however, be only between one-fifth and one-quarter of the per capita GNP of Israel. In the comparison of government consumption, because of the slightly increased developmental opportunities, this would also be some 18 per cent higher than under the status quo. There would also be an absolute improvement (some 23 per cent) in private consumption compared with the conservative scenario. Investment, mainly in housing, would be some 45 per cent higher than in the *status quo* option and reach nearly $1b., i.e. 30 per cent of the GNP. This represents a 5.8 per cent annual growth rate for the decade. The import surplus (nearly $1.2 billion) would still be about 38 per cent – an increase in absolute terms, but a slight reduction in percentage terms.

It is assumed that net transfers would be only slightly higher than in the conservative option. A greater difference would be generated for the GDP which would reach $2,610 million with a per annum growth rate of 5 per cent.

The number of housing units constructed in 1997 would reach 11,500 (a 4.4 per cent per annum growth) while the total number constructed in the decade would be some 100,000. At the end of the decade there would be 290,000 occupied housing units, a 2.8 per cent per annum growth, with a population density of 6.29. In general, the projections for this scenario are a definite improvement on the conservative scenario (see Tables 6.1.3 and 6.1.4). For example, there would be 6.29 person per household compared with 6.63; 3.1 rooms per dwelling unit vs. 2.96 and 2.03 persons per room vs. 2.24.

The rate of growth of the GDP in construction would be even greater at 6 per cent per annum. This would be nearly $120m. greater (at $457 million) than in the *status quo* option. It would reach nearly 18 per cent of the GDP, and in employment 13 per cent. The number employed in construction in the WB/GS would reach 28,000 workers. All in all, this is an improvement on the conservative scenario.

Note also that only in the first year of this scenario (1988) were disturbances considered. While this resulted in a decline in construction activity, this was assumed to be rapidly overcome under an improved development climate.

6.4 Development and Construction in a Separate West Bank/Gaza Entity

Of the three options outlined, a separate entity represents the most radical scenario for the Territories. It would involve a major quantum change in political, economic and social development. This, in the short run, can only come about under conditions of an agreement between Israel and the Palestinians.

While the establishment of a separate entity would result in a loosening of many ties with Israel, certain economic links, albeit in a modified form, would have to remain. These include non-sovereign land access between the Gaza Strip and the West Bank, access to employment in Israel, and mutual trade. Furthermore, the entity's economic links with Jordan, the Arab states and the rest of the world would be strengthened. It would be dependent on receiving considerable economic aid from both East and West, international bodies, repatriation of Palestinian funds (individual and organizational), and the Arab oil states. Although we estimate that some 600,000[12] refugees and expatriates would choose to return over the period of a decade, the actual number could range from as few as 400,000 to as many as 800,000. Furthermore, while it is assumed that a special arrangement for East Jerusalem will be negotiated, this is not further considered in this report. This whole scenario, in contrast to the conservative and reformist projections, represents a high degree of discontinuity. A development oriented-administration is assumed to be in power during this decade. In this scenario, for purposes of illustration, the intifada is hypothetically assumed to have ended by the end of 1988 and the major changes to start by early 1989.

The population (see Table 6.1.1) of the "new" entity will exceed 2.5 million by the end of the decade, representing an average population growth of 6.3 per cent per annum, a rate rather lower than Israel in its first formative decade. A similar proportion of the population is assumed to be in employment as at present. At the end of the decade (1997), there would be some 490,000 employed (18 per cent of the population) of whom around 420,000 (85 per cent) would be employed in the West Bank and Gaza Strip and 70,000 in Israel. This would contrast with the *status quo* scenario whereby 120,000 would be employed in Israel (40 per cent). The rate of growth for employment in the new entity would have to reach 9.2 per cent if unemployment is to be avoided. This also contrasts favourably with the growth rate during Israel's first decade.

The GNP for the area under consideration would grow by 8.6 per cent per annum, a rate not only lower than Israel's initial rate but also lower than Jordan's during the middle and late '70s and early '80s. Note that the maximum GDP growth rate will be 10.7 per cent which is also lower than in Jordan for the aforementioned period. The GNP will consist of 10 per cent government consumption, 80 per cent private consumption, 38 per cent investment, and an import surplus of 28 per cent. Israel had an investment rate averaging 35 per cent of its GNP for its first decade and a half. The highest rate of growth necessary to achieve these objectives would be for investment: 13.2 per cent (a rate achieved by Israel and Jordan for various extended periods) and government consumption: 10.6 per cent.

This would involve much external assistance and an import surplus of at least $1,380 million. The investment required is some $1,860 million in 1997 (with an average of less than one billion per annum). This can be obtained from remittances, domestic savings, Arab oil states, repatriation of Palestinian funds and other foreign aid, both public and private. Over the 10 years, the per capita investment per annum would only be some $500 – an achievable goal.

There would also be a marginally higher GNP per capita of 8 per cent as compared with the reform scenario, but significant over the conservative scenario (36 per cent). Per capita private consumption would be 26 per cent higher.

However, GDP per employed person would be slightly lower than in the conservative option. The GDP would exceed $4.4b. which is 69 per cent higher than in the reform option and well over double that in the conservative scenario. For GDP in construction the 1997 data shows (see Table 6.1.2) that at $875m. it is 91 per cent higher than the reform option and 159 per cent higher than the conservative option. Its per annum rate of increase would be 13.1 per cent. This would represent a major change from existing construction statistics although the growth rate is similar to the period 1968 to 1974. Construction activity would reach some 20 per cent of the GDP and involve 15 per cent of the domestic work force (58,000 workers). The GDP per worker would be the highest of any sector with over 130 per cent of average. This would still be considerably less than the rate in Israel.

During the decade, because of the return of possibly 600,000 refugees and expatriates, there will be a great need for additional housing units. Housing finishes would reach 28,000 units (up from 7,000 in 1987). The total number to be constructed during the decade would be some 200,000 units – or twice that of the reform scenario. There would then be 390,000 units, assuming a deterioration of 20,000 units during the period, with a housing density of 6.54 persons per unit. This latter is slightly higher than that of the other two scenarios – i.e. more crowded conditions are likely. The 390,000 housing units only represent basic minimum needs, which is less than the social needs.

The growth rate for housing units built would be some 14.1 per cent as compared with 13.1 per cent for the GDP in construction. This growth which would be one of the driving forces in the WB/GS economy would be similar to rates achieved in Israel in earlier years and for several years after the 1967 war. At the end of the decade, with the settlement task in an advanced state, there would be a gradual reduction, especially after most refugee camps were eliminated. Although we took maximum practical growth rates into account, these would be insufficient to solve all housing needs at a level higher than basic minimums over a 10-year period.

7. Concluding Remarks

Both Israel and the West Bank/Gaza area were parts of Mandatory Palestine before 1948. While Israel, with well over three-quarters of the area, has achieved a relatively developed status, the residual area has, despite a significant increase in per capita consumption under the first half of the Israel occupation (1967-1978), remained economically underdeveloped. This was the case during the Arab occupation by Jordan and Egypt and it has continued to be the case under the Israeli occupation since 1967.

The West Bank, an integral part of Jordan for 19 years, was largely neglected in development plans with priority given to the East Bank. Their (WB/GS) population actually declined between 1948 and 1967. Both residential and non-residential building lagged behind and the area built per worker was very low by any standard. In the Gaza Strip, under Egyptian control, the construction sector, in terms of its needs, was even more backward.

Following Israeli occupation, there was initially a further retreat in 1967 in the construction sector of both areas. Only in 1970 was the approximate 1966 level of construction nearly reached.

The rate of growth for both housing and total building starts exceeded 26 per cent per annum between the period 1968 and 1979, the final year of rapid development. However, the growth rate for the subsequent period, 1979 to 1986, was only 1.2 per cent per annum. The slowdown was even more marked in the Gaza Strip. This clearly marks the end of the building boom. There was a slight decline in building starts in 1987 and early statistics, based on cement consumption for 1988 indicate a further decline, probably due to the intifada.

Investment in the WB/GS areas is mainly in construction, construction investment is mainly in housing and housing investment is mainly private.

In terms of ownership of residential facilities, there have been significant increases in the Territories since the occupation. Nevertheless, the level remains below that of Israel, even if one only looks at Arab minority areas.

The productivity of the WB/GS construction sector, in terms of area built per worker, increased very rapidly between 1968 and 1979. After that it levelled out, but at a productivity (officially) superior to that in Israel.

The total of WB/GS labor in construction, both in Israel and the WB/GS areas rose rapidly between 1968 and 1974 (from 24,000 to 45,000). Thereafter (to 1986) it increased to 64,000. Since 1972, over 72 per cent of these are employed in Israel. Since 1981, construction represents around 25 per cent of WB/GS labor. Most of the construction labor are employees and these are paid more than the average wage. They are also more highly paid if employed in Israel. However, in Israel they are only paid around 40 per cent of Israeli wage levels and do not enjoy the same social benefits.

The non-residential and public sectors of building in the WB/GS lag behind residential and private building, especially in recent years.

While construction did increase rapidly for the first decade of Israeli occupation, there are in recent years, many barriers to development caused by the occupation.

In terms of relative scenarios, even ignoring the effects of the intifada, it appears that a continuation of the present social, political and economic policies would only result in slight development of the construction sector (i.e. the conservative scenario). Even if one allows for some improvement in the "quality of life" (i.e. the reformist scenario), these changes would be inadequate for their real needs. Note that a continuation of the intifada would result in a significant decline in construction. Only in the event of the establishment of a separate WB/GS entity (i.e. the radical scenario) would there be development to match the real needs of the people and the growth in population. (See Appendix 2 for an alternative scenario.)

Notes

1. Introduction and Objectives of the Study

1 Bahiri, Simcha, "Industrialization in the West Bank and Gaza," The West Bank Data Base Project, Jerusalem, 1987.
2 The indirect source for Jordanian and Egyptian statistical data for the period 1949-1967 for the West Bank and Gaza was Cohen, Abraham, "The Economic Development of the Territories - 1922-1980," Institute of Arabic Studies, Givat Haviva, 1986 (Hebrew).
3 The Central Bureau of Statistics in Jerusalem publishes an Annual – The Statistical Abstract of Israel – and a quarterly (or less often) on the Territories: "Judea, Samaria and Gaza Area Statistics (formerly the Administrated Territories Quarterly)."
4 The Economic Planning Authority of the Office of the Prime Minister, Jerusalem, published two works in August 1967: "The West Bank: A General Survey," and "The Gaza Strip and Sinai: A General Survey," which reviewed the economies of the Territories.
5 Central Bureau of Statistics, ibid.
6 One of the earlier and better-known works which dealt with the (single scenario) economic aspects of a separate Palestinian state was by Tuma, Elias H. and Darin-Drabkin, Haim, "The Economic Case for Palestine," Croom Helm, London, 1978.
7 Bahiri, Simcha, "Peaceful Separation or Enforced Unity: The Economic Consequences for Israel and the West Bank/Gaza Area," International Center for Peace in the Middle East, Tel Aviv, 1984; Bahiri, 1987, ibid.
8 Tuma and Darin-Drabkin, ibid.

2. Methodology, Projections and Statistical Notes

1 Economic Planning Authority, ibid.
2 Central Bureau of Statistics, ibid.
3 East Jerusalem has around 140,000 Arab inhabitants but was annexed to Israel in 1967 and since then neither the CBS nor others publish separate statistics for this area.
4 Population statistics are discussed in Appendix 1.
5 The intifada and its effect on construction is discussed in Appendix 4.
6 The author did not visit the occupied areas because of the difficulties generated by the intifada, but had visited the area prior to the intifada.

3. Background: 1948-1967

1 Metzer, Jacob and Kaplan-Oded, "Arab-Jewish Dualism and Economic Growth in Mandatory Palestine," Maurice Falk Institute for Economic Research in Israel, Jerusalem, 1985.
2 Bahiri, 1987, ibid.
3 CBS, ibid.
4 Ibid.
5 Ibid.
6 Ibid.
7 Cohen, Abraham, 1986, ibid.
8 Ibid.
9 Mazur, M. "Economic Growth and Development in Jordan," Westview Press, Boulder, 1979.
10 Ibid.
11 Cohen, Abraham, 1986, ibid.
12 National Planning Authority, 1967, ibid.
13 Ibid.
14 Cohen, Abraham, 1986, ibid.
15 Ibid.
16 National Planning Authority, ibid.
17 Lipshitz, Yaakov, "The Economic Development in the Administered Area," Ministry of Defence, Tel Aviv, 1970 (Hebrew) (p. 128).
18 Ibid.
19 Others have put the figures as high as 25,000 e.g. Tuma and Darin-Drabkin, ibid, p. 66; and as low as 12,500, e.g. Ben Shahar, Haim; Berglas, Eitan; Mandlak, Yair, and Sadan, Ezra, "Economic Structure and Development Prospects of the West Bank and Gaza Strip." The Rand Corporation, Santa Monica, 1971, p. 52.
20 Others have put the total area built as low as 100,000 sq.m., e.g. Bregman, Arie, "Economic Growth of the Administered Areas, 1968-1973," Bank of Israel, Jerusalem, 1975, p. 67.
21 Cohen, Abraham, 1986, ibid, p. 251.
22 Lipshitz, Yaakov, 1970, ibid.
23 Ibid, p. 128.
24 Benvenisti, Meron, "The West Bank Data Project: A Survey of Israel's Policies," American Enterprise Institute for Public Policy Research, Washington, 1984, p. 4.
25 Most of this paragraph is taken from "The West Bank and Gaza Atlas" by Meron Benvenisti and Shlomo Khayat, and published by the WBDP in 1988, p. 55-56.
26 Cohen, Abraham, 1986, ibid.
27 Ibid.
28 Economic Planning Authority, ibid.
29 Bregman, Arie, 1975, ibid.

4. Housing and Construction under Occupation: 1967-1987

1 Figures range from 200,000 to 250,000 refugees.
2 Van Arkadie, Brian, "Benefits and Burdens: A Report on the West Bank and Gaza Strip Economies Since 1967," Carnegie Endowment for International Peace, Washington DC, 1977, p. 12.
3 "Open bridges" refers to the policy first formulated in 1967 by Moshe Dayan to allow West Bankers to continue their former links with Jordan.
4 This was in keeping with the aims of the so-called Allon Plan.
5 Hilal, Jamil, "The West Bank: Its Social and Economical Structure: 1948-1974," Palestine Liberation Organization, Beirut, 1974 (in Arabic, quoted by Gharaibeh, Fawzi A., 1985, ibid).
6 Bregman, Arie, 1975, ibid, p. 4.
7 See Appendix 2.
8 Benvenisti, Meron, "1986 Demographic, Legal, Social and Political Development in the West Bank," The West Bank Data Base Project, Jerusalem, 1986.
9 While the West Bank and Gaza Atlas (WBDP) indicates that there were 67,000 settlers in 1987, the CBS Statistical Abstract states that there were 60,000 Jewish settlers.
10 CBS, ibid.
11 The source of all construction employment and building area statistics between 1968 and 1986 is the Statistical Abstract of Israel. Data for 1987 is from the Monthly Bulletin of Statistics of the CBS and from data published by the Ministry of Housing and Construction Monthly Bulletin.
12 Spector, B.I.; Kayvan, S.; Keynon, G.; and Harvey, W.; "The Economic Implications of a Middle East Peace Settlement: An Economic Development Model for the West Bank and Gaza Strip," CACI, Arlington, Virginia, 1978.
13 Based on information supplied directly by Nesher-Seher (Cement Marketing) Ltd. of Tel Aviv.
14 Based on International Labor Official Report (1981), p. 37, quoted in Gharaibeh, ibid, p. 52-54.
15 Gharaibeh, Fawzi A., 1985, ibid, p. 97.
16 The data on Gaza housing is a reconciliation between the CBS Statistical Abstract(s) of Israel and Sara Roy's "The Gaza Strip Survey," WBDP, Jerusalem, 1986, p. 136-137.
17 United Nations Conference on Trade and Development (UNCTAD), "The Palestinian Financial Sector Under Israeli Occupation," 1987, p. 37-38.
18 Kimhi, Israel, Reichman, Shalom, and Schweid, Joseph, "Arab Settlement in the Metropolitan Area of Jerusalem," The Jerusalem Institute for Israel Studies, Jerusalem, 1986.
19 Benvenisti and Khayat, 1988, ibid, are the sources for most of this paragraph.
20 Bahiri, Simcha, 1987, ibid.

21 Bahiri, Simcha, 1987: see Table on p. 74 based on UNIDO Survey of 1984.
22 Bahiri, Simcha, 1987, ibid.
23 Private West Bank Sources.
24 Based on direct information from Nesher-Seher (Cement Marketing) Ltd. of Tel Aviv and the author's direct research for that firm.
25 All the data for WB/GS cement consumption is based on the author's annual reports to the Nesher-Seher firm, "Forecasting and Analyzing Cement Demand."
26 In measuring building activity as it relates to cement consumption two-thirds the weight is given to area of building starts and one-third to building completions. The increase in cement consumption per square meter built averages around 1.6 per cent per annum. This technical coefficient is supplied by Nesher-Seher.
27 Bahiri, ibid to note 25.
28 Abu Kishk, Bakir and Ghurani, Izzat, "Housing" in "A Palestinian Agenda for the West Bank and Gaza," Edited by Nakhleh, Emile, A., American Enterprise Institute, Washington, DC, 1980.
29 Ibid.
30 Statistical Abstract of Israel, 1988, ibid.
31 The estimates used here are based on extrapolation of annual data for housing construction in the West Bank and Gaza. Also, Abu Kishk and Ghurani, 1980, ibid, were used, as was Sadler, P.G. and Abu Kishk, B. in "Palestine: Options for Development," UNCTD, 1983, p. 41-42. Much of their work is based on a study carried out over a decade ago by the Engineers Association of the West Bank and Birzeit University on housing in occupied areas. Kimhi et al. estimate of 35 sq.m. per room and 2.7 individuals in a room and 13 sq.m. per person, lead to the (under)estimate of 85 sq.m. per unit.
32 Benvenisti and Khayat, 1987, ibid.
33 Abu Kishk and Ghurani, and Sadler and Abu Kishk, ibid.
34 Benvenisti, Meron, 1984, ibid, p. 19.
35 Ibid, p. 20-21.
36 Ibid.
37 Kimhi, Reichman and Schweid, 1986, ibid, p. 65-74.
38 Ibid, English Summary.
39 Ibid. Note that there is a discrepancy between the Kimhi et al. data and CBS data as to size of household for the West Bank. The 1967 data shows less than 7.0 persons per household as compared to 6.5 in 1987.
40 Kimhi et al., 1986, p. 65-74.
41 Ibid, English Summary.
42 Benvenisti and Khayat, 1988, ibid.
43 Ibid.
44 Kimhi et al., 1986, p. 66.
45 Ibid, p. 67.
46 Ibid.
47 Benvenisti and Khayat, 1988, ibid.
48 Ibid, p. 112-113.

5. Barriers to Development

1 Bahiri, Simcha, 1987, ibid. The chapter on "barriers" was written after recent interviews with many factors including those in the West Bank and Gaza prior to the intifada.
2 Based on Bahiri, 1987, and data from the "Statistical Abstract(s) of Israel."
3 Awartani, Hisham M., "A Survey of Industries in the West Bank and Gaza Strip," Birzeit University, 1979.
4 Bahiri, Simcha, 1987, ibid, Chapter 7.
5 "The Palestinian Financial Sector Under Israeli Occupation," United Nations Conference on Trade and Development, 1987, p. 37.
6 Ibid, e.g. UNCTAD as well as independent study of CBS data.
7 Benvenisti, Meron, "1986 Report: Demographic Economic, Legal, Social and Political Developments in the West Bank," WBDP, Jerusalem, 1986, p. 32.
8 Ibid.
9 Ibid.
10 Ibid.
11 Ibid, p. 33.
12 Ibid.
13 Ibid, p. 33-34.
14 The Civil Administration jurisdiction includes all the civil powers of the military government excluding the authority to enact primary legislation. While the Civil Administration staff officers appear to draw their authority from the Military Government, they are also subordinate to Israeli civilian ministries. This in effect creates a double chain of command. For example, housing and road constructions are also subordinate to the Ministry of Housing and Construction.
15 Benvenisti, ibid, p. 34.
16 Ibid.
17 UNCTAD, ibid, p. 38.
18 Efrat, Yona, "Development of the Territories of Judea and Samaria," Bar Ilan University, Seminar Work in Hebrew, 1980.
19 Private communication from Meron Benvenisti.
20 Ibid, Benvenisti, Meron and Khayat, Shlomo, 1988, p. 60.
21 Ibid.
22 Ibid, p. 38.
23 Ibid.
24 Ibid, p. 109.
25 UN-ECWA "Industrial and Economic Trends in the West Bank and Gaza Strip," 1981.
26 Private communication from Nesher-Seher.
27 UNIDO, "Survey of the Manufacturing Industries in the West Bank and Gaza Strip," 1984.
28 Ibid.
29 Balassanian, Edward, "Policy Recommendations to Alleviate Housing Problem," Seminar Paper, p. 2, quoted in UNCTAD, 1987, p. 38.

6. Ten-Year Alternative Construction Scenarios

1 The effect of the intifada not only on the present but on the future is discussed in Appendix 4.

2 Variations of this option have been discussed in Bahiri, Simcha, 1974 (ibid) and Bahiri, Simcha, 1977 (ibid).

3 This number of returnees (600,000) has also been estimated by Mark Heller in "A Palestinian State – The Implications for Israel," Harvard, 1983 and by Bahiri, 1984 (ibid) and 1987 (ibid). Tuma and Darin-Drabkin (ibid) and the UNIDO (ibid) teams talk in numbers of up to three times this, but these may be politically biased estimates, or possibly targets. The UNIDO estimates are based on the work of Abu Kishk (UNCTAD: "Palestine Options for Development," Geneva, 1983). Admittedly the numbers could be as low as 400,000 or as high as 800,000.

4 In practice the conservative scenario is most likely to lead to a continuation of the intifada with consequently less development.

5 These have nearly been halted in the wake of the intifada.

6 While inflation in Israel and the Territories over the past three years has exceeded 60 per cent, the shekel was only devalued against the dollar by around ten per cent (mid-1985 to mid-1988). This makes the shekel overvalued.

7 See Appendix 1.

8 There are some indications, especially in the exaggerated consumption of cement that much unofficial building is underway.

9 Spector et al., CACI, 1978, ibid, p. 203.

10 Cement and more advanced finished and semi-finished products.

11 In 1987 U.S.$ terms.

12 See footnote No. 3.

Appendix 1

Demographic Aspects

For the most part in this report, official Central Bureau of Statistics (CBS) data as regards population have been used. Nevertheless, we are quite aware that these may be understated and a short discussion follows.

Based on a recent research project which included population sampling in the West Bank and conclusions stemming from a comparative analysis of Palestinian population statistics from several sources including the Interior Ministry (MOI) population registry, the Central Bureau of Statistics (CBS), and the Civil Administration's staff officer for statistics it was found that the official CBS figures are understated. (See "The West Bank and Gaza Atlas" by Meron Benvenisti and Shlomo Khayat: WBDP, Jerusalem, 1988). Note again that there was only one census ever undertaken in the West Bank (excluding East Jerusalem) and Gaza Strip in September 1967. In that census it was found that there were 985,600 inhabitants of the Territories of which 585,900 were in the West Bank. Since then two censuses were undertaken in Israel (1972 and 1983), but none in the Territories. The WBDP unofficially reports that:

"According to CBS figures for 31.12.87, the number of West Bank Palestinians was 858,000. MOI figure for November 1987 gave the total of 1,252,000. The difference of almost 400,000 persons is 46 per cent higher than CBS estimates. MOI figures are clearly too high, and the difference must be attributed to under-reporting of death and permanent emigration...While there is no argument on the rate of growth, it seems reasonable to assume that the actual figure for 'permanent residents' (i.e. including residents staying abroad for less than a year) of the West Bank is higher than CBS estimates and lower than MOI figures."

An unpublished field survey of the WBDP of 250,000 residents in more than 100 villages found that "present" residents amounted to 78.1 per cent of MOI figures (i.e.

977,000) and 113.9 per cent of CBS figures. In an alternative analysis, the WBDP survey found that the population (31.12.87) was 81 per cent of the present population registry (PR) or 1,014,000 persons, and if those abroad for less than one year are included, 89 per cent of the PR or 1,090,000 persons (the method of counting Israelis).

There are considerable regional differences between MOI population figures and survey figures – and these are not incidental. "In areas closer to Jewish population centers, Palestinian population growth is faster than MOI growth rates. MOI based estimates are the only source of information on population growth of Arab localities and internal migration. No official estimates on population distribution by sub-districts or even larger towns are available."

The survey suggests that by the year 2000 "the population could reach 1,383,000 persons, or 1,488,000 persons including those abroad for less than one year." These estimates are larger than the CBS high projection for the year 2002 because of the higher starting point. Despite the fact that the population of the West Bank and consequently the Gaza Strip is usually understated in CBS statistics, this agency is the only one to offer comprehensive statistics on population, households, housing and construction. The different forecasts or projections influence the role of the physical planner as it relates to possible land uses and the location of building activity.

The WBDP recent publication, "The West Bank and Gaza Atlas" updates population figures still further. The "permanent" population, which includes all Palestinians abroad for less than a year, of the West Bank (excluding East Jerusalem) in 1987 was 1,068,000. Incidentally, the CBS also uses permanent population for Israel. This is 25.8 per cent higher than the average West Bank population of the CBS of 849,000. In the Gaza Strip, the WBDP Atlas has population data for 1986, e.g. 633,000. If this is updated (by the recent CBS average growth rate of 3.4 per cent) to 1987, then there were 655,000 "permanent" residents in Gaza as compared to 555,000 noted by the CBS. The total 1987 WB/GS population is, therefore, 1,723,000 as compared with the 1,404,000 listed by the CBS. This is 22.7 per cent higher. Note that there are also 140,000 Palestinians in East Jerusalem. The average population of Israel (including East Jerusalem) in 1987, was 4,369,000, of which 782,000 were non-Jews, mainly Arabs. The total Arab population of Israel and the West Bank and Gaza was 2,505,000 as against 3,587,000 Jews, i.e. 58.9 per cent vs. 41.1 per cent. The respective CBS percentages are 62.1 and 37.9 per cent.

To sum up, the general trend is for a population growth-rate in excess of what the CBS data suggests, a trend to urbanization and urban building and a trend towards areas of concentrated Jewish settlement. This last point is based on findings that "paradoxically the Israeli 'creation of physical facts' by taking possession of land and building settlements in the Territories intending to increase the ratio of Jewish population, has the opposite effect of diminishing migration and increasing Palestinian population growth."

It is quite likely that building activity statistics are also understated. This is based on a recent survey of cement consumption in the Territories – later discussed in Appendix 3.

Appendix 2

The Bi-national Economy of Israel and the Territories:

A Theoretical Note

A. Bi-national Economy and Inequality

Creeping annexation which began with the occupation, 21 years ago, has transformed "Greater Israel" into a *de facto* bi-national state, albeit one controlled by Jewish Israelis. Nowhere has this transformation been more visible than in the realm of economic realities. Yet the debate about the scope, permanence and the degree of reversiability of the bi-national economy has never been settled. Part of the confusion stems from the fact that both proponents and opponents of annexation have used economic arguments to bolster their case. Yet there also exists a general theoretical problem of identifying the characteristics of a bi-national economy and defining the ways in which such a construct differs from other forms of economic integration. While there is no formal definition of a bi-national economy in the literature, we must formalize this concept.

An international economy usually refers to a world economy in which units of different sizes are characterized by a variable degree of integration. By its nature, a small economy is more integrated or dependent on a larger world or regional economy than a larger unit. The heterogeneity of internal subsystems gives the larger unit or system a higher degree of autarky and larger domestic market.

The smaller economy is more dependent on external trade. This does not necessarily lead to its exploitation by other units large and small, as the smaller system may be fully developed and enjoy favorable terms of trade. External trade, however, represents a large degree of its output and consumption. Smaller economies are therefore more dependent and more intensely integrated within a greater economic framework.

The same analogue can be used in describing a bi-national economy, except that the system involves only two contiguous or geographically mixed national units or entities. This pattern should be distinguished from two separate national unitary economies. A unitary economy is so fully integrated that the economic subsystems cannot survive without constant interaction. In a bi-national economy, separate, identifiable, semi-autonomous national economies may still exist as subsystems in a fairly integrated overall system. A bi-national economy is an integrated economy with a high degree of economic interdependence between the two ethno-national units involved. Obviously, the degree and effect of integration is unequal for each of the national entities and depends on the level of their development. If the larger unit is economically more developed, then its degree of dependence on the smaller, less developed unit is more limited. Clearly, this type of relationship prevails between the developed economy of Israel and the underdeveloped West Bank and Gaza Strip (WB/GS).

More developed economies, whether small or large, tend to enjoy more favorable terms of trade in economic transactions with less developed countries. Some analysts have developed the concept of dependency, whether investment, resource or trade-based to describe those relations which are characterized by unequal exchange between nations. This dependency is said to be the result either of formal imperialism (political control and/or military occupation by a dominant power), colonialism (control plus settlements by nationals of the dominant power) or informal imperialism (economic control through multinational corporate investment, unequal trade or other means).

Dependency can be a useful conceptual tool to understand the nature of a national economy. Though there are political and legal ambiguities to non-statutory bi-nationalism, economically speaking this relationship may be viewed in terms of core and periphery units. Core territories economically dominate their peripheral areas and may or may not be contiguous. The most pronounced feature of this bi-national economy is the developmental disparity between the two units. The Israeli economy is over 20 times the size of the WB/GS economy with a per capita income approaching five times the size of the WB/GS unit.

These disparities explain why the pattern of effects on each of the national units is radically different. The WB/GS, as we have demonstrated, is overwhelmingly dependent on the Israeli economy, involving over half of their total employment and consumption in both Israel and the Territories, and over a quarter of direct output. The impact of WB/GS on the Israeli economy is more limited and mostly confined to providing labor for agriculture, construction, manual service tasks, and some positions in industry. Only in Israeli construction does labor from the occupied Territories play a significant role.

B. Equitable Bi-national Entities

Continued Israeli domination is likely to have a negative effect on developing both the economy and the construction and housing subsector, i.e. the conservative scenario. A partial easing of such domination as in limited autonomy, would positively affect the rate of growth of the economy and construction, i.e. the reform scenario. An end to the occupation leading to separation, would free the productive forces and there could be a rapid rate of economic growth and construction, i.e. the radical scenario. Another option theoretically existing in dealing with such ethnic disputes is of some con-sociational arrangement between the two peoples involved such as a bi-national entity. Only an equitable bi-national entity could qualify for such power-sharing.

In this section we are neither assessing the advisability nor the likelihood of such an arrangement. We do, however, attempt to determine what such an arrangement could entail and its impact on the economy and construction.

In most con-sociational arrangements, equity in political and economic structures is assumed. Here we would also have to consider equity as regards immigration.

Political equity can be achieved by one of several possibilities, some of which are outlined below:

(i) full civic equality for all residents on an individual basis without considering their ethnic origin in a unitary entity;

(ii) establishment of autonomous non-territorial national frameworks for each ethnic group in a federal entity; and the

(iii) establishment of autonomous mini-cantons involving several for each group and possibly also the including of mixed cantons in a confederal arrangement.

Here the theoretical option of both Jews and Arabs moving towards a position of shared or joint rule, however remote, should be considered. Such a con-sociational constitutional system could be developed that could guarantee an equitable degree of participation in government and possibly veto power over certain types of decision for separate ethnic groups.

In an evolutionary scenario – say, over a decade – there could be gradual devolution from the Israeli-Jewish near monopoly of power to a system increasingly offering more rights to the Palestinian-Arab community until full equality is reached. In this gradualist scenario, the achievement of economic parity would depend on the attainment of political equity. While the effect on construction will initially be similar to that of the reformist (autonomy) option, it would gradually, as progress is made, move towards the higher growth rates of the radical (separatist) option.

In the (theoretical) event that political agreement was reached to establish a con-sociational entity with the aim of equalizing political, economic and immigration rights then the rate of economic and housing growth would likely approach that outlined in the radical scenario. There would have to be a concerted effort to use political mechanisms to overcome natural continuation and/or development of unequal relationships.

Among the equalizing steps to be taken is the extension of the "Law of Return" which applies only to Jews, to include all Palestinians and people of Palestinian descent. In that event, the number of Arab returnees would reach that outlined in the radical option (e.g. between 400,000 and 800,000). This "right of return" would involve rights to housing similar to that received by Jewish immigrants to Israel. These rights are central to achieving an equitable bi-national status.

While economic equality between ethnic groups should

be one of the objectives of a con-sociational administration, given other international examples and the large economic and social gap between the two communities, this would be almost impossible to reach. Nevertheless, the administration and economic organization would strive steadily to narrow the gap. A degree of devolution of central power in favor of separate ethnic groups could aid in achieving a more equalizing policy. It is, however, possible that in a binational entity the existence of a more advanced Jewish economy, if it were harnessed to equalitarian policies, would serve to spur growth in the Arab sector. Alternatively, an advanced sector could stifle progress in the less developed sector. Both are possible.

Appendix 3

The Intifada and Construction

At the close of 1987 (December), the mass disturbances began. These continue to this day and are likely to continue at varying levels for the foreseeable future. While the basic objective of the participants in the intifada is a "shaking-off" of Israeli rule, there is as yet no sign that the Israeli authorities will accede to their demands in the near future.

These disturbances have so far caused an estimated 20-25 per cent drop in the GNP of the Territories during 1988. Their impact (both direct and indirect) on Israel to date probably does not exceed 5 per cent of its GNP — by the author's calculations — although this is unevenly distributed.

In construction, in both the West Bank and Gaza area (as measured by cement consumption), there has been a drop of around 7 per cent during 1988 as compared with 1987. In Israel, despite reports of a decline in WB/GS construction labor of around 25 per cent, there has been no comparable drop in output. In fact, for the first three-quarters of 1988 (compared with the same period in 1987), there has been an increase of 10 per cent in building area (average of starts and finishes). For the first 9 months of 1988, in terms of average area in the 21 largest cities, the increase was around 15 per cent. Note, however, that there has been a significant and serious decline in building finishes which involve the more labor-intensive operations in contrast to building starts. This increases the stock of unfinished buildings. As regards Israeli cement consumption, for the first 10 months of 1988, there has actually been an increase in Israeli cement consumption. In the long run, while the effect of the intifada on Israel may be smaller than WB/GS construction employment statistics suggest, it is still serious. However, in the WB/GS itself the drop is smaller than expected because labor which does not appear for work in Israel, may be utilized in WB/GS construction activity.

While the economic effect in 1988 of the intifada on the WB/GS economy would exceed a 20 per cent decline (over 1987), the reduction in housing units produced is estimated to be far less than this. We, for the purpose of this paper, assume a 5-10 per cent reduction. The effect of the intifada on rates of growth from this 1988 base are most significant for the conservative scenario since it assumes a continuation of the "disturbances" albeit in a reduced intensity throughout the forecast period. For the other two scenarios, the intifada is assumed to cease after 1988.